The Golf Masters Series

Seve Ballesteros
with Robert Green

TROUBLE-SHOOTING

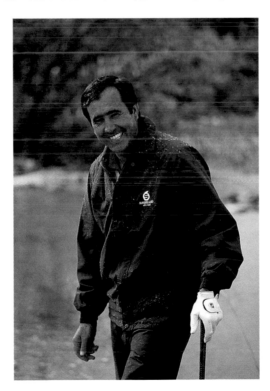

Photography by David Cannon

BROADWAY BOOKS New York

First published in the United States in 1996 by Broadway Books, a division of Bantam Doubleday Dell Publishing Group, Inc., 1540 Broadway, New York, NY 10036.

Produced by Roeder Publications Pte. Ltd.

Photography by David Cannon at Club de Golf Valderrama, Spain.
Rules of Golf © 1995 Royal & Ancient Golf Club of St. Andrews and the United States Golf Association

Broadway Books titles may be purchased for business or promotional use or for special sales. For information, please write to : Special Markets Department, Bantam Doubleday Dell Publishing Group, Inc., 1540 Broadway, New York, NY 10036.

FIRST EDITION

Printed in Singapore

ISBN 0-553-06164-X

96 97 98 99 00 10 9 8 7 6 5 4 3 2 1

CONTENTS

CONTENTS

INTRODUCTION

The first shot I saw Severiano Ballesteros hit was his approach to the 18th green at Royal Birkdale during the second round of the 1976 British Open Championship. It was a glorious July evening in Southport, and his match was one of the last out, among the expected also-rans, as the clock passed seven. There were no celebrity pairings for him in those days.

I was not alone in watching this conclusion to the day's play. The 19-year-old from northern Spain - "El Kid," as he was inevitably dubbed by some of the tabloids - had shared the lead after the first round with a 69. Now he had the lead to himself, and consequently the attention of the spectators, who had never heard of him 24 hours before; and the media, who, although he had topped the previous year's Continental Order of Merit, had not felt he was likely to do much this particular week.

After a huge drive at the last hole, then a par five, the golfing matador only needed a 5-iron to get home. His ball soared into the soft summer sky and found the heart of the green. Two putts later, he held a two-shot advantage at the halfway stage in golf's oldest championship. His closest pursuer was Johnny Miller, the golden boy of American golf, who told us - since the young man didn't even have an elementary command of English to do any informing himself - that his precocious rival was less formidably known as "Seve" and that, curiously, he was competing in this Open with a set of Johnny Miller-endorsed clubs.

A contemporary account of Seve that week described him as a "slashing player with a glorious, uninhibited swing, a talent for playing spectacular recoveries that his inevitably wayward driving makes necessary, and a wonderfully smooth putting stroke." Twenty years later, Seve's driving is still his weakness; his skills for recovery remain matchless.

He finished second in that Open, as Miller won by six shots. Three weeks later, Seve won the Dutch Open by eight. It was the first of what would be over 70 tournament victories worldwide, including the Open Championship three times and another of golf's four majors, the Masters at Augusta, twice.

Over the past 20 years, I have seen Seve hit thousands more shots, many of them rather less quotidian than a 5-iron to the middle of a green and several of them used in this book as a means of illustrating his transcendent talent for conjuring up breathtaking golf shots, of presenting the near miraculous as almost mundane, even in circumstances of intense competition.

There are many more shots to marvel in addition to those mentioned here. That Open of 1976 is remembered by many people not for Miller's win but for the wonderfully audacious chip-and-run that Seve hit to the final green, which bumped his ball between two bunkers and enabled him to make the birdie he needed to tie for second. Twelve years later, an equally deft touch from a fluffy lie beside the last green at Royal Lytham assured him of his third British Open title.

I also vividly recall the 1983 World Match Play Championship, where Seve was facing defeat in his first round match against Arnold Palmer. With Palmer one up and just through the green in two on the last at Wentworth, Seve's only realistic hope was to hole out for an eagle three and take the match into sudden-death. The problem was, he was about 20 yards short of the green and 40 yards from the flag. The solution was to hole the chip. He did, and then beat Arnie in overtime.

No golfing theater has regularly witnessed Seve in excelsis as much as the Ryder Cup. There was his incredible shot from a bunker on the last hole of his singles in 1983 (referred to in these pages); his inspiring the first defeat of the Americans for 28 years in 1985; his match-winning putt in 1987; the watching of him be all over the place yet play such a vital role in Europe's triumph in 1995. That's just a few of the top-line highlights.

Maybe the moment I especially regard as depicting vintage Ballesteros came in the 1991 Ryder Cup at Kiawah Island, in the match which the United States ultimately won when Bernhard Langer missed a putt of five feet on the final hole of the final singles.

The previous afternoon, Seve and Jóse Mária Olazábal, perhaps the greatest partnership in the history of the competition, were one down with four holes to play in the fourballs against Fred Couples and Payne Stewart. On the 15th, it seemed the Europeans were bound to win the hole to draw level. Stewart was in his pocket; Couples in a greenside bunker in three. Then, suddenly, he was in the hole in four - his trap shot had gone straight in. It had looked like Olazábal's four would secure the hole for Europe; now Seve needed to sink a downhill 15-footer for a winning birdie three. It was a potentially startling reversal for the Spanish pair, and the pressure was very much on whereas moments before there had seemed none, but somehow there was never any doubt that Seve would make the putt. Again, he did. The last three holes were halved and, with them so was that particular match.

That unwavering resolve is manifested in the quality of Seve's entire short game, and the never-say-die confidence it breeds helps to underpin his positive attitude to the difficult predicaments he often finds himself in on the course; the sort of situations he tries to help you with in this book.

You perhaps wonder if some of these shots really can be played by an average golfer. They can, believe me. I've done it - and there are many days when to call my golf "average" would be verging on unctuous flattery.

A few years ago, Seve explained to me how to play the parachute shot. He instructed me on the technique required to play what on first try seems a frightening risk - a full swing to send the ball a few yards. With my first effort, I thinned the ball into the bunker just in front of me. With my next attempt (honest!), the ball ended six inches from the cup - closer than any of Seve's earlier shots had finished.

I was thrilled beyond words. "There," said Seve cheerily. "See what I mean? It's not hard." But, equable as he was, he was equally determined not to be upstaged, even over something so trivial. He took back his sand wedge, dropped down another ball, and played the shot again. This time he holed it. That's another reason why he is such a successful trouble-shooter. He never gives up; he never thinks he's beaten. I guess the lesson is that neither should we give up.

"Sometimes it seems better for me to be behind a tree than in the fairway," he said one day when we were doing the photo shoot for this book at Valderrama in southern Spain. The words were uttered with a grin, but also with that deep, meaningful expression you feel he should patent. "Then I can see the shape of the shot I have to hit and what I have to do to play it."

After reading this book, here's hoping you can see how to hit a few of those yourself.

Robert Green

Robert Green

Fundamentals

REVIEWING THE SWING

I know, I know. You can't wait to get on to those dare-devil shots out of the near impossible lies I am going to talk about in this book. Indeed I expect you've already been flipping through the pages to see how the one-handed shot works. Most of all, you think you don't need a rehearsal to go over those basic instructions you learned some ten or twenty years ago. Let me tell you, there are many golf professionals who spend their entire lives between courses and practice grounds who become sloppy in the execution of their swings over the years and need some soul-searching and a good coach to put their game back together again. So let's test your knowledge a little before we move on to the exciting things that can be done with a properly polished swing.

You can't play good golf consistently if your game isn't built on sound fundamentals – a correct grip, solid stance, good posture and accurate alignment. Once you have these essentials ingrained in your swing through practice, your body will make the right movements naturally without you thinking about them every time you hit a ball. You then stand a fairly good chance of playing the shot you want, how and when you want to. Only then will you be able to benefit from the advice in this book and eventually lower your scores. However, if you set out to become a good trouble shooter without getting the basics right, you are trying to run before you can walk.

The Grip

The grip is the single most important factor for any golfer in producing a reliable swing that you can reproduce time after time after time. After all, the grip is the only contact you have with the club during the swing. It directs the clubhead throughout the swing and decides the success or failure of your shot. The type of grip you use is immaterial as long as you feel comfortable and secure with it.

Some world-class golfers have grips that don't conform to the most commonly used styles. For example, Bernhard Langer has a strong grip, with his hands turned clockwise from the normal position, while my Ryder Cup partner, José María Olazábal, has a weak grip. And these two players have won three Masters titles between them!

The Grip

Without a good, reliable grip, you can't play good golf. This is how you take it. OPPOSITE, FAR LEFT: Place the grip of the club in your left hand. BELOW FAR LEFT: Hold the grip predominantly in the palm and press your thumb against the grip, slightly to the right of center. BOTTOM FAR LEFT: The "V" formed between the thumb and index finger should be pointing straight to the middle of your chest, and you should see the knuckles on your index finger and middle finger. BOTTOM CENTER LEFT: Now the right hand comes onto the club. Here the "V" should point between your right shoulder and your chest. The only knuckle you should be able to see on your right hand is that of your index finger. LEFT AND BELOW LEFT: The little finger of my right hand rests beside the index finger of my left and the thumb and other fingers grip the club.

You may play your best golf with a grip that is not quite orthodox, as Bernhard and José María do, but they are exceptional golfers who spend their lives working on their games. If this isn't true of you, stick to the norm and give yourself the best chance of getting the most out of your swing as it is.

I use the overlapping grip, named after the great Harry Vardon, who popularized it by winning the British Open Championship a record six times. The majority of top players have adopted the Vardon grip. Others have opted for the interlocking grip, as did one of the greatest golfers of all time, Jack Nicklaus. Ladies, juniors and golfers with small hands might prefer it to the overlapping grip. Both grips are actually quite similar and are initiated in much the same manner.

Place the grip of the club in your left hand so that it is lying across your index and middle fingers. Then press your thumb against the grip, slightly to the right of center, putting it as far down the shaft as feels comfortable. This will cause the grip to rest predominantly in the palm of your hand. The "V" formed by your thumb and index finger should point straight to the middle of your chest.

Make sure that your hand comes naturally onto the club. Do not turn it too much to the left or to the right. Imagine you are about to shake hands with someone with your left hand. When it is firmly and correctly in place, you can see the knuckles of your index and middle fingers. If more than two knuckles are visible, then the grip is too strong. The hand position will then result in a closed club face through impact, causing a hook. If you can only see one knuckle - or worse, none at all - then your grip is too weak and the club face will open at impact, causing the ball to slice.

Let's look at the right hand now. With my overlapping grip, the little finger of my right hand rests beside the index finger of my left hand. The other fingers and thumb of my right hand wrap themselves around the grip of the club. For the interlocking grip on the other hand, the little finger slips between the index finger and the middle finger and rests across the former.

If you have followed my example, you will find that the "V" of your right hand now points between your right shoulder and chest. The only knuckle you should be able to see on your right hand is that of your index finger.

Last, but not least, have you given any thought to your grip pressure? Does it vary? Do you get tense under pressure and squeeze your grip when you tee off? Whenever you hold the club, do so firmly, but not too tightly. Hold the club as if you were holding a small bird, as Sam Snead used to say. Clutch it too tightly and you will squeeze the poor bird to death; hold it too lightly, and it will fly away.

Too little grip pressure will cause the club to slip in your hands and you will have no control over the shot. If, on the other hand, you hold on to your grip for dear life, you will create tension in your forearms. You will then lose clubhead speed and probably try to compensate by swinging too fast, which will only make matters worse. You need to exert just enough pressure to be able to control the club. You want to know how much is enough? I can't tell you that because every swing is different and every golfer needs a different grip pressure to control the club. The correct grip pressure for your swing is something you can only work out yourself.

The Stance

The set up puts your swing - literally - on a good footing. Without it, you can't swing properly. While stance and posture are essential for your game under the best of circumstances, they are increasingly important as the lie gets worse. We will see in the following chapters that the key to shotmaking in general and trouble-shooting in particular lies in the address position.

The most critical aspect in your stance is the distance between your feet. Personally, I set up with my feet shoulder-width apart, although other players favor a wider set-up position to increase their stability during the swing. That is a valid point, although I frequently see amateurs who overdo this and, as a result, find themselves unable to turn through the ball as much as they should.

In order to promote proper movement during the swing, flex your knees about 15 degrees, and bend your upper body forward as well, between 20 and 25 degrees. The precise angles for you depend on your height and build. You will find your right set-up position through practice. If you bend too far, you will be thrown off your feet when you hit the ball. If you don't bend enough, you won't be able to execute a proper turn.

Don't be discouraged if you occasionally make a mistake in your set-up; even the best players do so at times. How often have you read that someone like Nick Faldo or Greg Norman has attributed his poor performance to a faulty set-up? We professional golfers spend hours on the fundamentals of the game simply because they are fundamental.

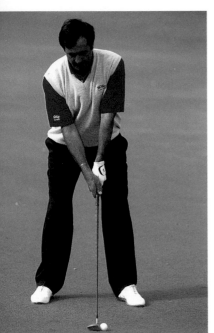

There are many different views on where the ball should be positioned in relation to your stance. Some people prefer to move the club backward in their stance as the clubs get shorter - maybe opposite the left heel with the driver and back in the middle of the stance for a wedge. Personally, I don't think that's a good idea simply because it adds an unnecessary variable to the equation.

Instead, I play the ball just inside my left heel for every club in the bag whenever I hit a normal shot. However, as you will see, the ball is played from a whole range of different positions whenever you have to shape and finesse your shots to get out of trouble. When playing a regular shot from a level lie, you only need to adjust the alignment of your feet. For the longer clubs (the driver down to the 4-iron), your stance should be slightly closed; for the 5-iron down to the 7-iron, it should be slightly open; and for the short clubs, your stance should be more open.

One aspect of the set-up position that regularly poses problems for high-handicap golfers in particular is the distance you should stand away from the ball. In my mind, the solution is simple. Once you have taken your stance, extend your left hand as far as you can while still feeling comfortable. Then, put the grip of the club in it so that the sole of the club is resting on the turf. That's how far away from the ball you should be.

When you have settled into your address position, your feet, knees, hips and shoulders must be parallel to the target-line. To hit the ball with a fade, some golfers set up with their feet aligned a little open to the target-line, or slightly closed, to produce a draw. But setting up in a position that feels most comfortable for you is likely to produce a consistent, accurate strike under all circumstances.

The Alignment

In the photographs on this and the opposite pages, you can see how I stand to the ball and also how I prepare to aim at the target. Alignment dictates the direction of the flight of the ball. Whenever you find yourself in trouble, more often than not, you have your alignment to blame.

To aim my shot properly, I first stand behind the ball and look at my target. Usually this is a point in the fairway or a part of the green, although, as you will see later in this book, it may also be an opening between two trees.

The Stance

TOP: *This is a good practice drill. Lay two clubs down in parallel on either side of the ball, pointing at the target. Now stand to the ball. You know the clubs are*

Standing behind the ball, I visualize an imaginary line between the target and the ball by first looking at the target and then drawing the invisible line back to the ball. Next, I walk up to the ball and put the club face behind it, holding the club in my right hand and making sure that the club face still points along the target line. Once I have gripped the club correctly with both hands and taken my stance, I look up at the target and check if the line is still as I first envisioned it. Only then am I ready to hit.

In the photographs here, I have laid two clubs on the ground on either side of the ball. This is a good practice drill if you find that your accuracy is awry. Stand behind the ball and look at the target, as you normally would. Then lay the clubs down parallel to each other, pointing at the target. Now take up your address position. If your stance feels uncomfortable, or your ball flies off the intended target line, you need to adjust your set-up. After a few practice sessions, your body should accept the correction and you will start hitting the ball straight again.

One final tip for your pre shot routine. Incorporate a waggle into your set-up procedure. Lightly move your body and the club back and forth at address to reduce tension. If you remain motionless over the ball for too long, your whole body will become too tight. This in turn will make it impossible for you to swing properly. Establish your own pre-shot routine and stick to it under all circumstances, from the very first hole to when you are putting to win the match. You will find that repetition pays dividends.

How did you fare in our little rehearsal of the fundamentals? Has your routine become a bit rusty and your address position a little sloppy since you last had a lesson? Practice the basics and you'll be well on the way to playing better golf. And even if you're not in top form, the following chapters should help you minimize the consequences of your bad habits.

pointing in the right direction. Flex your knees and bend your upper body forward a little. ABOVE: Your feet should be as far apart as your shoulders.

On the Slope

UNDERSTANDING GRADIENTS

I know of no place where amateurs make as many mistakes as on awkward hills and slopes. Some end up slicing patches of turf off hillsides with the club face without advancing the ball; others top the ball and then topple over themselves on their follow through.

High handicappers frequently find themselves on uneven lies in the rough. But even after a perfectly hit shot to the fairway your ball may not find a level lie, as anyone who has played on a British links course will tell you. Uphill, downhill and various combinations of sidehill lies require you to blend with the terrain. It's easy if you know how.

When I learned to play golf as a child, I knew nothing about swing technique, or gradients for that matter. All I know now I learned by trial and error, by hitting ball after ball out of ravines, steep hillsides, slopes full of rocks and uneven lies buried in high grass, covered with leaves and twigs. Sometimes, I played in the dark. In fact, I had only one club, an old 3-iron that belonged to my brother Manuel, and the first objects I hit were more often stones and pine cones rather than balls.

In that rather unorthodox manner I found out what worked and what didn't. I used my imagination and saw the shots in my mind so vividly that my body could feel what it had to do in order to achieve my goal and hit the ball out of trouble and back into play. It is very important that you use your imagination as well and approach those trouble-shots like an inventor with a challenging task.

Since you will find yourself under a tree, in deep grass, on a slope, under a bunker lip or in another player's divot every so often, it is vital that you always go onto the course in a positive frame of mind. If you think, "my ball is going to end up in the bunker over there", your body movements will almost certainly produce the (un)desired effect. We all have to go trouble-shooting sometimes. Be prepared to deal with the results of your more wayward or simply unlucky shots.

Above all, don't fight the slope. Let your body adapt to the contours of the land as much as possible so that you stand almost at a right angle to the ball just as you would on a flat lie. That way, you create the most solid foundation for your stance and ensure that you don't lose your balance.

You will feel more comfortable, play in a more relaxed manner and achieve a better score.

Slopes tend to put different spins on your ball, diverting its trajectory and affecting the length of its flight. As a rule of thumb, the longer the club or the steeper the slope, the longer the ball will fly through the air. Therefore, the more pronounced will the sidespin be on the ball. As a consequence, club selection is crucial with all uneven lies. Which way the ball moves depends on the type of the slope, as we shall see shortly. However, remember that you can never aim straight at your target from a gradient and you will always have to open or close your stance to compensate for the sidespin that the slope causes.

When it comes to playing shots from sloping lies, especially those that bring a combination of factors into play, many golfers have a problem finding the correct ball position at address. Depending on your individual swing, the severity of the slope and the shot you are trying to accomplish, it can range from nearly opposite the left heel to almost off your right foot. Here is a tip to help ascertain the right position for you.

Set up to play a practice shot just as you intend to address the ball in order to hit it. Make your swing, and note where the clubhead makes contact with the ground in relation to where your feet are. Now, when you get ready to play the ball, have the ball in the equivalent position in your stance to hit it as clean as possible.

The Uphill Lie

The ball tends to draw to the left from an uphill lie. To compensate, you need to aim a little to the right of the target. Again, the steeper the slope, the greater the draw will be and the more you must adjust your aim to offset the right-to-left spin.

When you take your set-up, the bulk of your weight should be on the right side. Your right leg will bend less and your left knee more than usual. Both legs should be flexed forward at the knee to enable a comfortable strike at the ball. Your shoulders should be parallel to the slope so that you stand at right angles to the ball. If you allow your body to find its balance naturally, you will be able to hit the ball as you would from a level stance.

When you address the ball in this manner, the line of your shoulders doesn't point to your target but way above it. In other words, your set-up

The Uphill Lie

Playing uphill, take more club to compensate for the fact that the ball is going to get up into the air quicker and aim right of your target to allow for the right-to-left ball-flight. OVERLEAF, TOP LEFT: *Set up with your weight mostly on your right side. Your right leg will be rather straight to carry this weight.* BELOW LEFT. *You will find you are forced to make a restricted hip-turn because of the nature of the slope.* BOTTOM LEFT: *As a consequence, the club will not be parallel to the ground at the top of the swing.* RIGHT: *Note how I have kept good balance coming down into the ball.* PAGE 23, TOP: *Make sure you stay down through the ball in order to make full, solid contact, resisting the tendency of the slope to force you up.* BOTTOM LEFT: *See how my eyes are still looking at where the ball was, even though it is by now well on its way.* BOTTOM RIGHT: *This follow through indicates that I have maintained good balance throughout the swing. It is how you should finish the shot.*

has effectively added loft to the club and the ball will fly higher and land sooner than you would expect. So bear in mind when you choose your club that a 5-iron shot from level ground becomes a 3- or 4-iron shot on an uphill lie, depending on the gradient. The steeper the slope, the more club you need to take.

I play the ball for all uphill shots from the center of my stance. You must find the most comfortable ball position for yourself, but avoid placing the ball forward in your stance, as this will put more loft on the club.

On the takeaway, your clubhead should follow the contour of the slope as far as possible to ensure that your vertical swing axis is perpendicular to the ball. As most of your weight is placed on your almost straight right leg, your hip turn on the backswing will be restricted, but don't try to force it.

Concentrate on staying behind the ball through impact. When you are playing from any slope, you may find it difficult to maintain your balance at first and consequently strike the ball less consistently than from a flat lie. Therefore, you may be anxious to see if you have hit the ball well and look up, pulling your body up along with your head. Remember to stay down through the ball longer than normal when playing from a slope, but don't let this stop you from making a complete follow through. As you can see in the photographs on pages 22 and 23, I have maintained good balance throughout the swing. You too should try to finish your swing like this.

One last word on uphill gradients: if the slope is particularly steep and you are keen to keep the ball down as much as possible - for example, below the branches of a tree, or out of a strong wind - you could play another, more upright shot by leaning into the slope, not with it. In that case, you need to hit the ball with the low, punching action I shall describe in more detail on page 106.

The Downhill Lie

A downhill lie poses a greater problem for most golfers than an uphill lie. As with the uphill shot, you need to set up as nearly perpendicular to the gradient as possible. This posture will again affect the angle at which the ball flies off. The slope effectively delofts your club and makes it difficult to get the ball airborne. If you are in 6-iron range from the flag, you should take your 7-iron from this position or even an 8-iron if the downslope is sharp. Although you are using a more lofted club, on landing the ball will run farther than it usually would when struck with the same club.

The Downhill Lie

OPPOSITE: *Take a more lofted club than normal and aim to the left of the target. The majority of your weight should be on your left leg.*
OVERLEAF, LEFT TO RIGHT, TOP TO BOTTOM: *Your swing will naturally be a little steeper than normal from a downhill lie. Swing within yourself. Standing at a right angle to the slope at address will have programmed the necessary compensations into your swing. Make a specific effort to stay down on the shot, through impact and beyond. Do not try to lift the ball into the air. The lofted club that you have selected will do that job for you. Work on completing your swing in balance and with a full finish.*

OPPOSITE, LEFT TO RIGHT, TOP TO BOTTOM: *When the ball is lying above your feet, choke down on the grip so that the top portion juts out above your hands. Aim your feet as well as the club face to the right of the target. Just as the slope will make the ball fly left of where you are aiming, so it will make your swing assume a flatter plane than usual. You can see here how I have narrowed my stance to counteract this effect, making me stand taller, and also how my right foot is drawn just a little behind the left.*

A ball played from a downhill lie tends to fade, so aim to the left of your target. Again, the fadespin increases with the gradient. Only practice will teach you how far to the left you need aim to compensate for a particular type of slope.

Visualize where you want the ball to hit the ground in order to have it finish where you want it to, but don't be so ambitious as to imagine that this shot can cut into the green and drop like a feather next to the flag.

With your body at right angles to the ground, you naturally need to place most of your weight on your left leg. Remember to keep your knees flexed. The ball position is a little forward of center so that you don't slap the club into the hill instead of hitting the ball. Take the club away along the outline of the terrain to ensure that you are on the right swing plane. Like for the shot from an uphill lie, the downhill gradient restricts your hip turn and leads automatically to a somewhat steeper-than-normal swing.

Again, you need to make a specific effort to stay down during the swing, since it is all too easy to top the ball from a downhill lie. Quite a number of golfers make the mistake of trying to lift the ball into the air off this slope. You don't need to do that. Remember, that's why you have taken a more lofted club than normal. Just stay down through the ball and let the club do the work for you.

The Ball above the Feet

When the ball is above your feet, you need to make several adjustments to your usual set-up. But once you have altered your address position, you can make a normal swing.

First and foremost, choke down on the grip so that a bit of the butt end of the club is showing above your glove. This is necessary because the slope on which the ball is nestled has effectively moved the ball closer to your club. You need to compensate for this difference if you don't want to hack into the hillside behind the ball instead of hitting it.

Aim your feet - not just the club face - to the right of the target. The slope of the ground will tend to shape the flight of the ball from right to left, because the club touches this gradient with its heel only, resulting in a closed club face at impact. How much to allow for the diversion in the ball's trajectory is determined by your choice of club and the steepness of the slope. In the pictures on page 29, the side slope is not especially severe,

The Ball below the Feet

RIGHT: *With the ball below your feet, grip the club near the top of the shaft so that you can reach down to the ball more easily. Aim your body and club face to the left of the target to compensate for the effect of the slope.* BELOW RIGHT: *The slope will naturally make your swing more upright than normal. Make sure you stay behind the ball through impact and keep a good balance throughout the swing.* OPPOSITE: *Maintain that balance to the finish. Take extra club for this shot to allow for the left-to-right shape of the shot.*

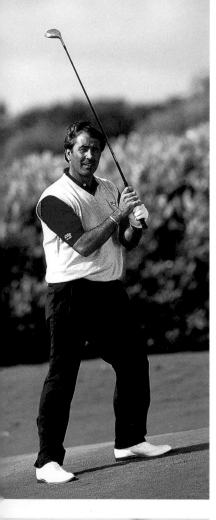

so I'm using a pitching wedge. If I were to use a longer club, I would aim even farther to the right, just as I would if the slope were steeper.

With the ball above my feet, I must swing on a flatter plane than usual. To offset the effect of the shallow swing plane, I narrow my stance so that I stand as tall as I can to the ball - even though I am gripping down on the shaft. You should do this, too, to swing from as upright a position as possible under the circumstances. This adjustment will help you to control the club better and, by delivering the club face to the ball at as steep an angle as possible, also prevents the ball from veering off too low.

Keep your right foot a bit behind the left as you address the ball. This position will feel more comfortable for the necessary shallow attack on the ball. Position the ball itself in the center of your stance, a little farther forward if you are using a longer club and a bit back if you take a shorter club. Have your weight evenly balanced between your feet and pushed a little forward toward your toes.

For a shot from any kind of incline, especially a sidehill stance, starting out with and maintaining a good balance throughout the swing is vital. You can't hit a good shot if you are about to topple over, or are afraid that you will any time soon.

A lie with the ball above the feet often induces golfers to move their body across the line of the shot, causing a huge cut at the ball. This invariably leads to an ugly swing and a predictably bad result. Instead, take the club wide around your body to ensure that you are on a shallow swing plane to complete your backswing. When you come down and through the ball, you want to swing with a sweeping action, a feeling of swishing the ball away rather than hitting down sharply into the back of it. And don't forget to complete your follow through.

The Ball below the Feet

This shot is not an easy one to execute and requires numerous adjustments before you can play it, starting with your club selection. In the photographs on pages 30 and 31, I purposely chose a 3-wood to get some extra distance.

With the ball below the feet, the toe of your club tends to hit the ground first on the downswing, resulting in an open club face at impact. This will send the ball on a left-to-right trajectory, which curtails the distance the

The Ball above the Feet Uphill

OPPOSITE, FAR LEFT: *From an uphill lie with the ball above your feet, choke down on the grip to increase your control over the ball and to be able to take a more comfortable stance.* CENTER LEFT: *Note that here the ball position is in the center of my stance.* LEFT AND BELOW LEFT: *Allow your body to compensate for the lie of the land, with your head and the center of your body as the axis of your swing.*

The Ball above the Feet Downhill

OVERLEAF, TOP LEFT: *There are two conflicting inclines in play here, so you must make sure that your stance feels comfortable.* BELOW LEFT: *The ball should be forward of center in your stance and your right foot should be drawn back.* BOTTOM LEFT: *Having got the set-up right, you can make a full swing at the ball.* FAR LEFT AND PAGE 35: *Stay down through the shot and let the power of your swing carry you to a full finish.*

ball flies. The slope, which causes a steep swing plane, adds to this effect. Therefore, choose one or even two clubs more if the slope is steep so that you won't leave the ball short. A longer club will also help you reach down to the ball. As a result, your set-up will feel more comfortable and you will swing better.

All shots played from any sort of slope require a solid, balanced stance. When the ball is below your feet, you should address it with your feet slightly wider apart than you normally would. To have a stable foundation for your swing, place your weight more toward your heels. Since the slope has, in effect, moved the ball farther from you, you will need all the length in your club that you can get to reach down to the ball, so you will have to grip it near the top of the shaft. Then position yourself to the ball as you normally would.

When you take your stance, you must compensate for the fadespin on the ball by closing your stance and the club face. The more pronounced the slope and the longer the club, the greater the tendency of the ball to curve off to the right, because the longer the ball spends in the air, the more time it has to stray off its line. In other words, if you are a 5-iron shot away from the target, as opposed to just a wedge away, you will have to aim farther left when you set up.

The closed address position, with the right foot drawn back a little, also ensures that you will stay behind the ball through impact rather than coming off the shot, which is what will happen if you lose balance. While a shot with the ball below the feet will naturally fade, any mis-hit will cause the ball to stray severely to the right.

The Ball above the Feet Uphill

Since you are dealing with several variables at the same time, the first decision you must make whenever your ball finishes in an uneven lie is to decide which single factor is dominant. Is the ball severely above your feet while the downhill slope is gentle? Or is it the other way around? You will then need to adjust your stance primarily to the more prominent slope.

The overriding factor you will need to take into consideration will depend on the exact circumstances of the lie. For example, if the ball is above your feet, you will impart drawspin on your ball. But if you are also on a downslope, you will also impart fadespin on it as well. If the two gradients are equally steep, then the different sidespins may offset each other and the ball may fly straight unless you naturally draw or fade the ball with your normal swing. Generally, the more prominent slope will determine the prevailing sidespin in this situation.

From an uphill lie with the ball above your feet, a well-hit shot will certainly draw, and maybe even hook. Both slopes encourage the ball to fly from right to left. However, unlike the usual draw shot from a level lie, the ball will not travel farther than normal. Both the upslope and the sideslope will cause the ball to fly higher and therefore shorter than you would expect. Depending on the severity of the two slopes, take a 4- or even a 3-iron to get the yardage of a 5-iron on level ground.

Since the ball is above your feet, go down on the grip as you hold the club to avoid hitting the sidehill. By doing this, you will also be more comfortable at address. Then, position yourself so that the ball is in the center of your stance.

As with all these types of shots, let your body compensate naturally for the lie of the land so that you can swing freely, with your head and your body - as the axis of your swing - perpendicular to the slope. Don't follow the example of many amateurs and tilt and sway back and forth during your swing in the vain hope that all will come right at the moment of impact. It might work once in a while, but generally such tactics only cause you to lose power. They will certainly guarantee that you never achieve any consistency. I think you will see that the balanced finish I have obtained here is a testimony to the good balance I have maintained throughout the swing. That is what you should attempt to achieve as well.

The Ball above the Feet Downhill

In this case, we have the effect of two conflicting sidespins to contend with. The fact that the ball is above your feet will curve the ball from right to left. The downslope, on the other hand, will impart a fadespin on the ball. As before, the more severe slope will tend to dictate the direction of the shot you want to make.

With the ball above your feet, you need to narrow your stance again to get the ball up in the air and so you place more weight on your toes. Allow your body to find a position in which you feel totally comfortable. Then grip down on the club and make the flat swing necessary for this kind of sidehill slope.

Off this downhill lie, place the ball slightly forward in your stance to get through it better at impact. Draw your right foot back just a hair

The Shot on Tiptoe

BELOW: *Go down on the club so that your right hand is actually holding the shaft itself.* RIGHT AND BELOW RIGHT: *Note how much to the right of the target I am aiming here because the ball will fly immediately left after impact. Open the club face wide. You need to have room to swing at the ball while maintaining your balance.* FAR RIGHT AND BELOW FAR RIGHT: *Keep your arms moving through the swing, although gripping the club so low on a slope like this will curtail your swing.* OPPOSITE: *Hit through the ball after impact - do not quit on the shot.*

The Left-Handed Shot

RIGHT: *Take a left-handed grip, with your left hand below the right and your bottom hand actually on the shaft of the club. Put your weight largely on your right side. Aim well left of where you want the ball to finish.*
BELOW RIGHT: *The swing is short, and made mostly with the hands.*
OPPOSITE, TOP: *Hit the ball with a sharply descending blow.*
BELOW: *You can get a sense here of how the ball is immediately flying to the right after impact.*

behind the line. As before, this position will encourage you to stay down through the ball, which is one thing you must strive to do with every shot, whatever the shape of the slope you are standing on. Again, note the balance I have kept into a full, free finish.

The Shot on Tiptoe

I once had to play a shot like this in the Madrid Open. I don't remember the year, but I remember the shot all right. I had to stand in a bunker to play the ball perched well above my feet. In fact, on that occasion it was almost opposite my head.

The whole point here is not to stretch too much. Allow your arms to hang naturally. Go down on the club so that your right hand is actually holding the metal (or graphite, if that's what your irons are equipped with) of the shaft, not the grip itself. You will then have enough room to make an unrestricted swing at the ball.

The key to playing on tiptoe is to feel comfortable and secure in the stance. You need to stand up to the ball as tall as you possibly can. Although this posture may look unconventional, it is a pre-requisite for attempting this shot. This stance will force you to make a proper swing at the ball rather than just turning the club around your waist, without any body coil and therefore without much power.

With your weight being so far forward, it needs to be evenly distributed between your feet. Otherwise, you could easily lose your balance. To offset the effect of the slope on the direction your ball will fly, you have to aim well right of the target. The ball is sure to fly immediately left after impact from a stance like this.

Open the club face to counteract the inevitable drawspin of the slope and the effective delofting of the club caused by the flat swing plane. The open club face will send the ball up into the air after impact.

The Left-Handed Shot

The left-handed shot - although a real stroke-saver in many cases - is awkward enough to play under any circumstances, but nowhere is it as tricky as from this lie. Therefore, I sincerely hope that you don't routinely end up on steep gradients, leaving you either the option to venture this shot or take a drop under penalty for an unplayable lie. But you always want that to be the option of last resort. However difficult the shot might be, I firmly believe that if you can make a swing at the ball, there is no shot that cannot be played.

Reverse your usual grip by placing your left hand below the right. Overlap or interlock as you usually would. Go well down on the grip, depending on the severity of the gradient, so that you have enough room to make a proper swing.

In the photographs on pages 40 and 41, you see that my bottom hand is actually on the shaft of the club, not the grip. Due to the angle of the slope, you will need to set up with your weight predominantly on your right leg. You will not have to think about how to take your stance, your body will do it naturally.

Aim as much as 45 degrees left of your target. This is necessary because the toe of the club rests on the ground at address, which will cause the club face to close at impact, forcing the ball to fly well right of what you are aiming at.

The swing should be short, and made mostly with the hands. Hit the ball with a sharp blow, letting the wrists break just a little through impact. As it is not an easy shot to master, remember to practice it well before playing it on the course. A couple of practice sessions will give you a valuable tool to avoid a penalty drop in this situation in the future.

The Ball below the Feet Uphill

In such a position, you are again facing two opposite forces. From an uphill lie, the ball tends to draw, while a ball position below the feet results in a fade. The fadespin, however, is more often than not the dominant factor in this shot, so aim left of your target. How much you need to adjust your alignment depends on the extent of the respective slopes. Only by working on this aspect of your game will you get a better feel as to how the ball might react in such circumstances.

Take a club more than you would for a shot from an even stance as the uphill slope will curtail the distance of the shot. The uphill lie will also induce you to place your weight on the right side. To accommodate the sidehill, with the ball below your feet, widen your stance a little and take your grip towards the end of the club. Regardless of the upslope, you won't be able to play this shot with a shortened grip. And remember to draw

The Ball below the Feet Uphill

LEFT: *Take more club than usual for this shot to allow for the slope and for the ball position. Widen your stance. If you take the correct set-up, you can make a full swing. Maintain your balance at all times and you, too, can finish your follow through with a flourish.*

draw your right foot somewhat behind your left at address so that you stay behind through impact.

The Ball below the Feet Downhill

This lie means that conflicting issues have to be resolved. Since you are hitting from a downhill lie, you theoretically need less club than you normally would. However, the ball will fade because it is below your feet. Therefore, you may need to take more club. Either way, make sure you aim well to the left with this shot.

To stay behind the ball throughout the swing, draw your right foot just behind your left at address in order to help you get the desired inside line of attack into the ball. Also, widen your stance a little to give you a solid base for an upright swing. As with the regular downhill shot, your weight should be more on the left hand side at address. Grip the club longer than normal. Place the ball forward in your stance, as you did for the normal lie with the ball below your feet, to make room for your swing.

The Ball below the Feet Downhill

OPPOSITE, FAR LEFT: *As with the regular downhill shot, your weight should be more on the left side at address. Note how my right foot is drawn just behind the left to help me stay behind the ball through impact.* LEFT: *The takeaway is quite flat, both because of the incline and the wider stance.* BELOW FAR LEFT: *Make a full turn until the club is parallel to level ground at the top of your swing.* BELOW LEFT: *Through impact, stay down on the shot. If you can turn your right hand over the left on the follow through you have got through the ball properly.*

In the Sand

BUNKER STRATEGY

One of the biggest problems facing most golfers is their mortal fear of bunkers. Some amateurs appear perfectly scared whenever their ball ends up in the sand. They freeze over the ball, all tense and tight, and as a consequence, get predictable if unsavory results. It is hardly surprising then that they emerge from the sand with worse bunker blues than they went in. Let's try to break this vicious cycle.

You are probably familiar with the essential points of playing a simple sand shot, such as setting up with an open stance with the club face slightly open, taking the club back outside the line and hitting down sharply into the sand between one and two inches behind the ball. Of course, this all depends on how far you want the ball to travel through the air and how big a swing you intend to take.

What follows involves some variations on the above, but the fundamentals stay the same. Make sure you always take a firm stance, wriggling your feet into the sand to give yourself a solid base from which to play the shot. Never ground the club, whether it be your sand wedge or any other club, prior to playing the shot. If you do, you will incur a two-stroke penalty.

Before I help you escape from some awkward places in the sand, especially around the green, I should say one word about strategy. When you are stuck under the lip or face a tree between the bunker and the green, you won't necessarily be thinking about how close to the pin you can get the ball, even if you are a proficient bunker player. But as the following example shows, it doesn't hurt if you do.

A shot from a fairway bunker paved the way for me to win my first major championship, the 1979 British Open at Royal Lytham. Everyone still remembers the shot I played from the car park at the 16th hole on the final day to set up the birdie that virtually sealed my victory. However, what happened three holes earlier was even more important.

The 13th at Lytham is a fairly short par four, under 340 yards, that dog-legs to the right. I was tied for the lead in the championship, and there was the small matter of Lytham's notorious five finishing holes to come. On the 13th, the wind was behind us, and I tried to drive the green. However, I was unlucky. My ball just caught one of the cluster of traps on the right-hand corner of the dog-leg and went well down in the bunker. The lip was high - typical of Lytham's bunkers. On the other hand, the lie was reasonable and I could get my pitching wedge to it.

The distance to the flag was some 70 yards. It was a tough shot, but I was young - only 22 then - so I was not afraid of attacking the pin. The shot was almost perfect, and you know how seldom even top professionals hit perfect shots in their rounds. The ball hit the green pin-high, but the spin I had put on it caused the ball to finish about six yards from the pin. You can imagine my disappointment. It was short-lived, however, as I proceeded to hole the putt and take the lead. Five holes later, I had won by three strokes.

But these are the finer points of bunker play. The main objective of trouble-shooting in sand is to get out. That way you will at least get down in three more shots, and if you are lucky and sink a good putt, maybe just add two strokes to your score. That reminds me of what my good friend Gary Player, perhaps the greatest bunker player the game has ever known, likes to say: "The more I practice, the luckier I get." If you include awkward bunker shots in your regular practice sessions, you might find that you get down in two shots more often than three. And who knows, even now and then, you might even hole one!

The Downhill Lie

Remember the principles for the shot from a downhill lie we dealt with in the preceding chapter? You must align your hips and shoulders parallel to the contours of the sand. Don't fight the slope.

Due to the nature of the gradient your left leg will bear most of your weight. Notice how flexed my knees are in the photographs on pages 52 and 53. Play the ball off your right foot so that you don't dig the clubhead into the sand. Whereas for a routine shot from a level lie, I tend to keep my upper body a little behind the ball, I move it slightly ahead of the ball for the downhill lie in the bunker to get through the sand and pop the ball out at impact.

Choke down a bit on the grip and open your stance a little to the left of the target with your body, but aim the club face at the flag or any other target you may have. From an awkward lie like this, you may not be able to attack the pin and may have to go for another part of the green. Remember, the main objective is to be putting with your next stroke.

The Downhill Lie

OVERLEAF, TOP LEFT: *The key to this shot lies in allowing your weight to follow the slope of the sand, which means most of it is on your left leg. For this shot, the upper body is behind the ball, which itself should be played off the right foot.* BELOW LEFT: *On the takeaway, cock the wrists quickly, opening the club face even more. This shot requires a steep, upright swing.* BOTTOM LEFT: *Do not keep your body weight behind the ball. Going through the ball, your body should follow the shot. You want to feel that you are chasing after the ball with your right hand.* PAGE 53: *Keep the club low through the shot.*

For the downhill trap shot, open the club face at address slightly - as is normal from most lies in the sand - but don't overdo it. If you open the club face too much, you risk hitting the ball with the leading edge or else burying the whole club in the sand. Either way, the result will be grim.

On the takeaway, cock your wrists quickly. The nature of the slope will force you in any case to make this a steep, upright swing. Use your practice swings (no touching the sand, though!) to make sure that you will not catch the back of the bunker on your backswing.

Going through the ball, your body should follow the shot downhill. Don't keep your body weight behind the ball, as with a normal shot. If you do that, you will either hit too far behind the ball, probably leaving it in the sand, or else you'll top it, sending the ball into another bunker on the other side of the green. Feel as though you are chasing after the ball with your right hand. Keep the club low through the shot.

The ball will fly out lower from a downhill than from a level lie in the sand, so beware of any significant lip of the bunker before the green which it will not clear. The ball will also run a longer way on landing, so allow for the roll if you hope to finish close to the flag and prevent it from rolling over the green on the far side.

This downhill bunker shot is perhaps the toughest trap shot you will encounter with any regularity on a course. But work at it, and then when you're facing the sandy downhill lie out on the course, commit yourself to the shot. A half-hearted execution will only increase your chances of having to play from the sand again with your next stroke.

If you can play sand shots with a 3-iron, as I had to do on the beach in Spain because it was the only place I could practice, you can deal with most of the problems found in a bunker. But even for me, the downhill bunker shot is no cinch. One of the best I ever played was at the 1988 Manufacturers Hanover Westchester Classic in New York, the month before I won my third Open Championship at Royal Lytham.

The tournament went to a playoff between Greg Norman, David Frost, Ken Green and myself, starting from the 10th hole at the Westchester Country Club, a dog-leg left par four of 304 yards that could be reached with a good drive. My brother, Vicente was caddying for me at the time. I wanted to use my 3-wood after Frost and Green had driven into trouble, but Vicente thought I should hit the driver. It almost got on the green, but instead finished in the front bunker - on a downslope.

I remember the bunker I found my ball in as if it all happened yesterday. It was an especially tough downhill lie which I had to address with my left foot in the bunker and my right foot out of it. I struggled to find my balance but eventually managed to play the shot as I just described to you. The ball flew off and landed within five feet of the hole. When I sank the putt for a birdie three, I had won the tournament for the second time.

The Shot from the Lip

If you make a mess of a downhill bunker shot, the ball will scuttle across the sand and end up under the lip of the trap. When the ball is tucked as close to the lip as this, you will have to follow my example and hit the ball standing outside the trap.

The key to playing this shot properly is to hit very hard with a steep, sharp blow down on the ball to get it up very quickly. You also want to strike the sand closer to the ball than you would with most bunker shots. The correct ball position to escape from a bunker lip is just opposite the inside edge of your left heel.

In common with many other bunker shots, the feet and body should be aligned to the left of the target, although the club itself should point more to the right of the flag than for a normal sand shot. From this position, there is less risk of you thinning the ball or hitting too heavily behind it, and you want all the elevation you can get.

The open stance will help you to produce the out-to-in swing that you need to get the ball up into the air in time to clear the lip of the trap. In conjunction with the open club face, this address position will send the ball in the direction of the flag.

To facilitate the steep swing you need, cock your wrists quickly. Since your body weight is mostly on your right side, there is little body turn or leg action in this shot, and your hands will not go much past waist height. The escape from a bunker lip is a right-hand dominated shot. It turns under the left hand as you go through the shot. The flange of the club is the part that strikes the sand first. The proximity of the lip of the bunker will naturally restrict your follow through.

The Shot from the Lip

OVERLEAF, LEFT: *Open the club face more than you would for a normal sand shot. Most of your weight should be on your right side.* RIGHT: *Cock your wrists quickly in order to achieve a steep swing plane.* PAGE 57, LEFT: *There is little body turn or leg action in this shot, meaning that the backswing will be curtailed.* RIGHT: *The right hand controls the shot. Strike the sand with the flange of the club, and hit it very hard just behind the ball. The ball, in contrast, should come out softly.*

The Buried Lie

This is certainly something you don't want to see as you walk up to a green. Your high approach shot has just missed its target, but now your ball has plummeted into a buried lie in a bunker. Don't panic. The key to playing this shot lies in the angle of the club face at impact with the sand. This is why you have to make so many changes from your set-up for a regular bunker shot.

Instead of being open at address, the club face should be square. Since the ball is lying more deeply in the sand than normal, a square angle of attack is necessary to dig the club deeper into the sand in order to make sure the ball comes out. The worse the lie, the squarer the club face should be. In the photographs opposite, my feet, knees, hips and shoulders are all square to the target to have a better chance of hitting the ball with maximum impact.

Take a fairly open stance, as you would for a normal bunker shot, with your hands ahead of the clubhead. But this time, place your weight much more on your left foot to encourage the sharp, hard, downward blow you want to give the sand in order to extricate the ball from the buried lie. Place the ball slightly more toward your right foot than normal to allow for the steeply descending swing you are about to deliver. You may also want to go down the grip a little in order to gain greater control over the clubhead for this violent stroke.

Start the swing by cocking your wrists as much as you can, taking the club back very steeply. Coming down, strike the sand two inches behind the ball, hitting it very hard, and make sure you stay down throughout the shot. Remember, you must dig deeper for this shot.

Since you have entered the sand at such a sharp angle, you will find that your follow through will be abbreviated. If you have played this shot properly, the clubhead stays stuck in the sand. As with the bunker shot from a downhill lie, you will not be able to impart spin to the ball from this lie and the ball will run a long way on landing, so aim at the widest part of the green.

If the buried lie is a particularly bad one, consider taking the pitching wedge rather than your sand wedge, especially if the sand is packed hard. You may find that the sharper leading edge of the former makes it easier for you to slice into the sand to force the ball up and out. With the pitching wedge, place your hands even more in front of the clubhead than usual.

The Buried Lie

OPPOSITE, LEFT: *Take a fairly open stance, with your hands ahead of the clubhead. Concentrate your weight on your left side, with the club face square to the target, and the ball near your right foot.* BELOW LEFT: *Take the club back very steeply, cocking your wrists sharply. Then strike the sand, very hard, two inches behind the ball.* BOTTOM LEFT: *Stay down on the ball through impact.*

The Shot to a Tight Pin

OVERLEAF, LEFT: *Open your stance more than for a normal bunker shot, although the club should still be pointing at the flag. Stand a little wider than usual, too.* CENTER: *Going back, cock your wrists early. The way you have set up will give you the desired out-to-in line of attack into the ball.* RIGHT: *The right hand is the dominant one in this shot. As you strike the sand - perhaps only half an inch behind the ball in this case - it should rip under the ball, creating the spin that will get it to stop quickly.*

The Shot to a Tight Pin

This is the bunker shot that all amateurs wish they could play better, especially when they see professional golfers in tournaments walk serenely into the sand, flick the ball out and stop it on a penny. That illustrates the point that tour professionals are generally happier in a bunker than on the grass around a green.

You don't want to hit as far behind the ball as you do with many bunker shots, because you want to put spin on it, and the closer the club gets to the ball, the more you can spin it. Bear that in mind as you take your set-up.

Open your stance more than for a normal bunker shot, although the club should still be pointing at the flag at address. Stand a little wider than usual in order to feel more comfortable in this exaggerated position. The wider stance will stabilize your lower body and encourage your hands to stay low through the shot to apply as much spin as possible. For the same reason, choke down on the grip a little. The ball is played from the center of your stance.

On the takeaway, cock your wrists early. Make a normal swing, relying on the way you set up to the ball to make the club cut across the line from out-to-in as it comes down to make impact with the sand.

The right hand is the dominant one in this shot. As you strike the sand - perhaps only half an inch behind the ball in this case - it should rip under the ball. With practice (that word again!) you will become comfortable playing this shot, being at first amazed and then confident about how full a swing you can make and yet have the ball fly such a short distance.

Exactly how far you send the ball will depend on the speed of your swing and how far down the shaft you grip the club. The slower the swing and the lower the grip, the shorter the ball will travel. But however far the ball goes, it will stop quickly when it gets there.

The shot to a tight pin is a vital one in the repertoire of any professional. I have no idea how many times I have played such a shot when it really mattered, but one occasion that does stick in my mind was a rather bitter-sweet experience.

At the 1989 Masters, I had completed my third round on Sunday morning (rain having interrupted play on Saturday afternoon) by making birdies at three of Augusta National's last five holes. When I birdied the first hole of the final round, I was only two shots behind the leader, Ben Crenshaw. At the 2nd, a par five, I was just short of the green in two and still short in three. I had dumped my pitch shot into the bunker protecting the right side of the green.

I was quite close to the front of the trap, and the pin was close to the front of the green. All in all, I was perhaps only 20 feet from the hole. The lie was a good one, and I hit the shot I have just described. The ball came out softly, landed just short of the flag, and rolled sweetly in for an unlikely birdie four.

Unfortunately, I didn't go on to win a third green jacket. That was the year Nick Faldo won his first after Scott Hoch missed a short putt that would have won the Masters for him on the first extra hole. This shows that you need more than one lucky break to win the Masters.

The 5-Iron Sand Shot

The idea of using your 5-iron from a bunker may seem preposterous, but on some occasions, it's simply common sense. You could find yourself in a similar predicament, as you see me in the photographs overleaf, often enough to merit some practicing of this shot. You don't think so? How many times have you found yourself in trouble, having to get the ball over one obstacle and under another? More than you thought at first, I'll bet.

This bunker is beside the 5th green at Valderrama on Spain's Costa del Sol. The course is due to stage the 1997 Ryder Cup and has been rated the best in continental Europe. At first sight, this shot might seem X-rated. It need not be so.

Your sand wedge, the conventional club for getting out of bunkers, offers no solution here. It can get the ball out of this trap for you all right, but only if you are prepared to take a risk by hitting it through the tree or else playing safely away from the green, out to the left. Either way, you'll do well to get down in as few as three shots, and it may take you four. My 5-iron shot, on the other hand, almost guarantees that the job can be done in three, or on a good day, and with practice, maybe even two.

The 5-iron will get the ball up sharply enough to get over the lip of the bunker and yet keep it low enough to stay under the branches of the tree. Because you have to make some allowances for the comparative lack of loft of the club, the technique here calls for you to take the club back on an exaggeratedly outside path. You need to have the club face well open at

The 5-Iron Sand Shot

OVERLEAF: *Because you are using a 5-iron, you need to create loft on the club. Open the club face as I am doing here, and have your body aligned well left of the target, although the club face itself is still aimed at the flag. PAGE 65: Take the club back on an exaggerated outside path, again cocking the wrists sharply on the takeaway. PAGE 66: From the top, prepare to cut across the ball on the pronounced out-to-in swing path that your set-up has programmed. PAGE 67: Strike the sand between an inch and an inch and a half behind the ball. After impact, follow the club around to the left with your body, keeping your hands well behind the ball as it goes toward the flag.*

The Fairway Bunker Shot

RIGHT: *If the lie is good, the lip is not too high and you need to get the distance, you can play as much as a fairway wood from a bunker. Make sure you have a firm footing in the sand and hover the club behind the ball at address. Remember - you can't ground it in the sand!* BELOW RIGHT: *You want to be swinging within yourself, as I am here, not trying to make an extravagant swipe at the ball. Have your weight a little more on your left side to promote the steeper plane necessary to catch the ball before the sand.* BOTTOM RIGHT: *If you have made all the appropriate adjustments, you can play this just like a shot from the fairway. Make a full swing at the ball. As with all shots from sand, tentativeness tends to get you nowhere except in more trouble.*

address to compensate for the lack of natural loft. But don't open the club face by shifting your hands around on the grip. In other words, take your grip normally and then open the club face.

You must align your body much farther to the left here than you would for a normal bunker shot, although you can see that the club face is pointing at the flag. Into the swing, cut across the ball, hitting between an inch and an inch and a half behind it. After impact, follow the club around to the left with your body, keeping your hands well behind the ball.

I think one of the main differences between myself and other tournament professionals is that although we can all play a vast array of shots, I always try them out on the course and in competitions, and don't just leave them on the range. That goes especially for short-game shots and I believe that sometimes gives me an advantage over my rivals. While the quality of golf at your club may not be of the same standard as it is on tour, you can certainly give yourself an edge over your playing partners and opponents if you work on shots like this.

The Fairway Bunker Shot

Finally, let's look at the difficulties facing you when you have a good lie in the sand but the green is a long way away. The thought of having to play a long bunker shot is a nightmare for many club golfers. It should not be. In the photographs opposite, I am facing a really long fairway bunker shot which I address with a 3-wood. That's how comfortable you can be playing a shot like this.

Before using a long club from a fairway trap, however, a word of caution: make sure the lie is good. (If not, then play out with a shorter club to a spot on the fairway from where you would like to hit your next shot.) Ensure you have enough loft on the club to get it over the lip of the trap.

Once you have decided which club to take, make sure you have a firm footing in the sand. One of the most important things about this shot is to keep your body from moving too much during the swing.

Bear in mind that you won't hit your career-best distance with any club from a fairway trap. You want to be swinging within yourself to make certain you make good contact with the ball. This is not a time to try hitting it out of your shoes.

Hover the clubhead over the ball at address, taking care not to touch the sand. Place your weight more on your left side than normal in order to achieve the steeper arc necessary to catch the ball before the sand. If you catch the sand first, then the ball will go no distance at all.

Even though in this case you are playing a wood, you want to strike the ball with a more descending blow than you would from the fairway. All the good bunker players, like Jack Nicklaus for instance, use an upright swing for a shot like this. Make a full swing at the ball, just as you would from the fairway. Anything less and your caution will probably cause a mis-hit.

My best ever shot from the sand was the one from a fairway bunker at the 1983 Ryder Cup. I was all-square on the last tee of my singles match against Fuzzy Zoeller. The 18th on the Champion Course at the PGA National in Florida is a long par five. I was in deep trouble - in a bunker, 245 yards from the flag, and I had already played two shots. I felt that Fuzzy was going to do no worse than make five, so somehow this shot had to go on or near the green if I was at least going to halve the match.

Under normal circumstances, the most ambitious club I would have used in that situation would have been my 5-iron. However, these were no ordinary circumstances, and I chose my 3-wood, the only club that could get me on to the green.

I was lucky in that the ball was on a slight upslope, which meant I could get it up above the lip of the trap more easily. However, I still had to open the club face to get the ball up in time. I also had to aim a little to the left of where I really wanted to go to give myself a bit more room to get the ball airborne. But hitting that bit of a fade meant that I would lose distance, and there was a right-to-left cross-wind to contend with as well. All in all, it was a very tough shot to attempt, and very risky, too.

Fortunately, I got the ball close to the green and made my par, as did Fuzzy, and we halved the hole and the match. Unfortunately, it wasn't enough to prevent the United States from beating us by one point to retain the Ryder Cup.

Europe's day would come two years later at The Belfry. But I still remember that afternoon in Florida as being the day I hit one of the best shots of my life. The American captain, the great Jack Nicklaus, described it at the time as "the most incredible golf shot I have ever seen". I have to admit that praise doesn't come much higher than that!

Deep in the Grass

HANDLING THE ROUGH

Contrary to what some people think, I don't spend all my time in the rough. I have played enough shots from the short stuff to appreciate that you want to be in the fairway as often as you can and leave the thick grass for the flora and fauna. But golf isn't always like that, of course. In my last round of golf in 1995, against Tom Lehman in my Ryder Cup singles match, it wasn't until we reached the 10th hole that I actually hit a fairway off the tee.

However, even when your ball goes into the bushes, don't despair. Even though the only target I had found from the tee on the front nine against Tom Lehman at Oak Hill was the green on the par three 3rd hole, at the turn I was only one down and had gone out in one over par. For the record, when I did split the 10th fairway, I knocked my approach shot into a bunker, but we did halve the hole in pars.

The following are seven examples of rough lies and situations you might expect to encounter with some frequency on the course, from far out and from close to the green. If you can utilize the advice here, you won't necessarily relish hitting your ball into the rough, but I hope that you won't be walking up to it every time with such trepidation.

The Flyer Lie

When the ball is sitting up in the rough, and you are about to play a shot in the same direction as the grass is growing, you are faced with a flyer lie. From this position, the ball will carry farther than normal, and run more on landing, because you can't impart any backspin on the ball since blades of grass will inevitably get between the clubhead and the ball at impact. So although you're in the rough, take one club, sometimes even two, less than you normally would. For example, you might find that your 7-iron will go as far as your 5-iron usually does, and certainly as far as your 6.

The set-up for a hit from the flyer lie is similar to the address for a normal fairway shot. After all, you have a good lie - maybe even too perfect a lie. However, since the ball is going to fly farther than normal from it, there are a couple of adjustments you need to build into your swing for this shot.

To offset the loss of control over the ball due to the grass getting between it and the club face, set up with an open stance with the ball forward in it,

Grassy Lies

TOP: *With a good lie in the rough, you might be able to have a go with a fairway wood, or a long iron.* ABOVE: *From a bad lie like this, don't attempt to hit anything more ambitious than a medium iron.*

with the club face squared to the target. What you are trying to do is hit the ball higher than normal to compensate for the distance the ball will run when it lands.

The Shot against the Grain

When you find the grass growing directly against your intended line of flight, the ball is likely to be lying down deeper in the grass, so you need a lofted club to get it out. On the other hand, the ball is clearly going to fly less distance from this lie than it would from the fairway, so you may be tempted to take more club to compensate for this. Don't, because a less-lofted club will often send the ball nowhere since it will be smothered by the grass. So what should you do?

It was Billy Casper who used to say, "if the lie isn't good enough to get a 4 wood at the ball, don't try anything longer than a 5-iron". That's sound advice in most circumstances. Depending on the lie, you may even use a more lofted club out of the rough, not one that you think will give you greater distance. I suggest this for three reasons:

1. The greater loft on the club will enable you to get through the ball better.

2. It will make sure you get the ball airborne, and the quicker the ball clears out of the rough, the farther it is going to travel.

3. The rough will tend to close the club face, making it effectively less lofted than usual anyway.

Of course, everything depends on your commitment to practice. Only experience will tell you what you can achieve under the circumstances and how the ball will react to your technique.

Although the lie with the grain against your shot direction is in many respects the opposite to the flyer lie, the ball will again run on landing, rather than stop quickly. This is because again blades of grass will interfere with the clubhead at impact and there will be no backspin on the shot.

The set-up here should see you with the ball a little bit back in your stance in order to promote the sharply descending angle of attack you want. Your swing needs to be more upright than for a shot from the fairway or from a flyer lie so that you come down into the ball more steeply. On the downswing, you should feel as if you are holding the club behind your

The Non-Flyer Lie

TOP: *In the non-flyer lie, the ball is lying with the grain of the grass against your intended target line.*

The Flyer Lie

ABOVE: *A flyer lie has the grass growing in the same direction as you wish to hit the ball.*

The Shot against the Grain

ABOVE AND OPPOSITE, ABOVE RIGHT: *When the grass is lying against you, you need to place the ball back in the stance to make a good swing at it.* ABOVE FAR RIGHT: *Take a more lofted club to get the ball airborne and have your hands slightly ahead of the ball on the takeaway and throughout the swing.* CENTER RIGHT: *You need to swing in a more upright fashion to generate a steep angle of attack on the ball.* CENTER FAR RIGHT: *Get down sharply.* RIGHT: *The ball will head left after impact.* FAR RIGHT: *Notice my high follow through.*

hands. With this sort of lie, you want to dig the ball out of the rough, and the steeper swing will ensure that the clubhead is hindered less by the grass before impact than would otherwise be the case.

Aim right of your intended target, because the ball will travel left as a result of the closing of the club face at impact when it is caught by the grass. If you are trying to extricate yourself from thicker rough or heather - that gorgeous looking purple plant found on many British courses that is sheer hell to escape from - the ball might snap sharply left. Remember to allow for that.

Finally, let's go back to Billy Casper and the possibility of using a wood from the rough. That might be a safe shot from a flyer lie, but it's not usually suitable if the grass is growing against you. However, if the ball is sitting up on top of the grass, effectively nullifying the effect of the grain running against you, you might well be able to get a wood at the ball, just as if you were playing it from the fairway. But remember not to get too ambitious in the rough when you are all excited about having a good lie against the odds.

The Shot from Long Grass

However far you have to go to get to the green, when the rough grass is very thick, perhaps so thick that you can scarcely see your ball, there is no sensible alternative to using your pitching wedge or sand wedge. Whichever one you choose depends on your preference of club and on the nature of the lie.

Say you have 165 yards to the green, and that would normally be a 5-iron shot for you. If you use your 5-iron from a lie like this, all you'll do is hit the ball 20 yards and probably still have it in the rough. The club simply doesn't have sufficient loft to get the ball airborne.

Suppose you opt for your 8-iron instead? That's better, but it is a risky ploy. There's still a chance that you might not get the ball out and on to the fairway. In any event, you won't reach the green or even get close to it.

So why not use one of your wedges, knock the ball out 60 or 70 yards, and leave yourself another full wedge shot onto the green from the fairway, which is just about the most straightforward shot in golf? On average this is unquestionably the sensible thing to do.

We all like to play heroic shots and to pull them off. Believe me, I have probably attempted more audacious shots than most golfers during my career, and maybe I have succeeded with a higher percentage of them than others, but it's vitally important to know what you can and can't do. So accept the fact that the lie is bad and play the hole in as few shots as possible. The lie in the long grass may ultimately mean that you have to settle for turning a possible par into a comfortable bogey. Just don't turn it into anything worse.

We now come to the swing. Since I have conceded that it is not going to be possible to get to the green from here, I'm going to concentrate on getting the ball out to a suitable spot in the fairway. From a lie in deep grass, you want to play a punch shot that comes out low - the lie rather dictates that anyway - and hot, almost fizzing out to the place you have selected in your mind's eye. You don't want it to come out low and feeble, which probably means your ball will flop down in the long grass a few yards farther on. This shot may be like a punch, but it needs to be like one of Mike Tyson's.

Because the ball is so deep down in the rough, you need to hit it with a very steeply descending action. Play the ball between the center of your stance and your right foot. Your weight should be more on your left to help create that steep swing you need.

Have your hands well ahead of the ball at address in order to promote the upright swing plane. You might want to grip the club a touch firmer, with your left hand in particular, to prevent the grass from twisting the club face at impact. In order to reduce the chances of the clubhead getting snagged by the turf at the start of your takeaway, hover it over the ball rather than place it behind it. Few things ruin a swing so thoroughly as an interrupted takeaway, and I'm sure you've played enough golf to know how hard it is to stop your swing once you're in motion. I also like to close the club face slightly at address, despite the lie, because I find that that also improves your chances of getting the club back to the ball unimpeded by the rough.

Cock your wrists early in the takeaway. The steeper-than-normal swing you need to make here will lead to a shorter turn of the hips and shoulders. The fact that your weight is more on the left side will have the same effect. Then all you have to do is hit the ball hard.

The nature of the lie and your hand position ahead of the ball will effectively take loft off the club, so take that into account. When you take aim, remember that the ball will fly to the left of your target because of the

The Shot from Long Grass

ABOVE: *Take an 8-iron or an even shorter club.* OPPOSITE, ABOVE RIGHT: *Play the ball between the center of your stance and your right foot. Your weight should be more on your left side. Also, have your hands well ahead of the ball at address.* ABOVE FAR RIGHT: *Cock your wrists early in the takeaway.* RIGHT: *Hit the ball hard.* FAR RIGHT: *The position of my follow through indicates that this is a punch-type shot.*

The Pitch from Long Grass

RIGHT: *Choke down on the grip and open the club face slightly. Your weight should mostly be on your left side, and your feet closer together than normal.* OPPOSITE: *Take the club back on an outside line. Cock your wrists early and make a shortened backswing. Come steeply into the ball, hitting the ground a couple of inches behind it.* OVERLEAF: *Through impact, don't let your right hand cross over the left.*

slightly closed club face. So adjust your alignment accordingly to the right. The thicker the grass, the farther right you need to aim.

The Pitch from Long Grass

The pitch from long grass is a shot that we often encounter in the US Open, where the greenside rough is as thick as it can get. The technique for playing this shot is similar to an explosion shot from a bunker, although at least here you can ground the club since you are not in a hazard.

In contrast to many of the other shots in this book, this is a gentle one. You should feel as if the clubhead is dropped in behind the ball, not slammed in there. But like many of the other shots here, it requires a good deal of practice before you can feel confident enough to employ it.

Choke down on the grip to control the club better, holding it just above the shaft. A suitable club for this shot is your sand wedge, although you can also play it with a less-lofted club if you don't have to clear a hazard immediately in front of you.

Place your weight more on your left side and open the club face slightly. Stand erect to the ball with your feet closer together than normal. The ball should be just a little nearer to your right foot than for a regular pitch shot of this length.

Take the club back on an outside line. Cock your wrists early and make an abbreviated backswing of three-quarter length. Come in steeply, hitting the ground a couple of inches behind the ball and sliding the clubhead underneath it with the right hand, which mustn't cross over the left. The important factor for this shot is hitting behind the ball, not at it. If you attempt to catch the ball first from this lie, you will simply skull the shot and leave it in the rough.

You won't have much of a follow through, but the ball will run on once it hits the green, since there will be no backspin. Take that into account when visualizing where you want the ball to land.

The Downhill Shot out of the Rough

In the photographs illustrating this shot on pages 86 and 87, you will see how my body has adopted the dictum about never fighting the slope. My weight is very much on my left side and my upper body is forward, as if trying to catch up with the slope. This position encourages the steeper backswing that you need and ensures that the club face is kept lower through the shot.

The ball is in the center of my stance. I break my wrists early, to get the steep plane that I want. Note that this is only a short swing. After all, you're not trying to hit the ball a long way. You can almost tell from the pictures on page 86 that I have got the ball to pop up nicely out of the grass, and the other photograph emphasizes the low follow through as I chase the ball forward.

Even if you make perfect contact, you must take into account that you are, first, playing downhill and, second, playing from the rough. Both these factors will tend to make the ball run on landing. You must plan the landing area of this shot carefully to have it finish close to the hole.

Above all, stay within your capabilities. If you try to be too ambitious, you could find yourself playing your next shot from the rough again.

The Parachute Shot

The parachute is a wonderful stroke-saving shot for your short game. Use your sand wedge to play it, and the ball will fly high and short, and land softly. Once you have the parachute in your armory, you will find it highly useful for many occasions.

When you are in the rough, with a hazard between you and the green and no place for you to run the ball, the parachute shot comes in handy. It's your stroke-saver whenever you are not thinking of attacking the hole but rather of just landing and keeping the ball on the green. Whenever a routine pitch is either going to leave the ball short of the bunker, in it, or over the green, take out your parachute. Also known as "the floater", this shot can get you down in two from a situation where many people have trouble getting down in less than four.

First, open the club face and take a very open stance. Play the ball forward in your stance, opposite your left heel. Concentrate your weight on your right side so that almost the entire weight of your body is on the right foot. This uneven weight distribution effectively adds loft to your club, which is what you need here. To increase that effect, place your hands behind the ball at address.

To start your swing, take the club back on a steeply upright plane and outside your usual swing path. Cock your wrists as much as you can on the

The Downhill Shot out of the Rough

LEFT AND OPPOSITE:
Let your body go with the slope. You can see that my weight is very much on my left side and my upper body is leaning forward. Make a steep backswing, breaking the wrists early. This is only a short swing. The follow through on this shot should be low, following the slope as you chase the ball forward.

takeaway. Coming back down, the feeling I like to have is one of my right hand being "under" the ball, going on through it on a pronounced inside line through impact.

This is distinctly a right-sided, right-handed shot, and if you execute it properly, your right hand will lead your knees, hips and upper body into a finishing position facing down the line of the shot.

It is important to hit this shot hard. Don't be scared of taking a full swing to hit the ball a comparatively short distance. If you chicken out and try to finesse the ball, you will either hit it heavily and it will not reach the green, you will knock it into a bunker, or you will thin it over the back.

Like the 5-iron from a bunker, once you've practiced this shot, don't be afraid to try it on the course. Only that way will you learn to trust your swing and allow the loft of the club to do the job for you.

Talking of mastering this shot reminds me of one time I used the parachute shot to great effect - in the first round of the 1994 Masters. As you may know, there is almost no rough at Augusta, and on this occasion my ball was in fact on a clean, tight lie, which made the shot harder to play.

I was on the 4th hole, a longish par three, when my tee shot missed the green badly on the right. With 25 yards to the flag, and a big bunker in between, I took my sand wedge and played the parachute shot. Even though the green was sloping away from me, the ball stopped four feet above the hole.

It would have been criminal to have wasted the shot by missing the putt, but I didn't. My playing partner that day, Raymond Floyd, himself a winner of the Masters and three other major championships, was generous enough to say afterwards: "That was the most fabulous par I've ever seen."

The Bellied Wedge

This excellent shot can be employed easily and to great effect from just off the green instead of using your putter or attempting a chip. The bellied wedge comes into its own especially when the ball is lying tight against the collar of rough around the green.

Take your sand wedge, choke down on the grip to improve your control over the shot, and address the ball with your club pointing right at its middle. In other words, don't ground the club. It's better to hover it

The Parachute Shot

LEFT: *Set up with an open club face and a very wide stance. Place the ball more forward in your stance than for a normal pitch shot - about opposite your left heel. Concentrate your weight on your right side. Your hands should be slightly behind the ball.* BELOW LEFT: *Take club back on a steeply upright plane and outside what would be your usual swing-path. Cock your wrists as much as you can on the backswing.* BOTTOM LEFT: *Coming down, you should feel as though your right hand is going under the ball. Your right hand will lead your body through the shot. Hit the shot hard, and use a full swing, leading to a complete finish.* PAGES 90-93: *The steep swing plane follows an outside-in path.*

behind the ball in order to reduce the risk of snagging the clubhead in the grass on the takeaway. Unlike most shots, this is not one where you intend to strike the bottom of the ball.

Instead, hit the equator of the ball firmly with the leading edge of the club, employing a stiff-wristed stroke. It's almost as if you were trying to hit a deliberate top. The ball will roll toward the hole, just like a putt.

Practice this shot to get a feel for how hard you have to strike the ball in order to make it go specific distances. You will soon find that you are getting down from the fringe in two, or even one, with greater regularity.

The Bellied Wedge

ABOVE: *Do not ground the club firmly at address.* ABOVE FAR LEFT: *Choke down on the grip of your sand wedge and address the ball with your club pointing at its equator.* ABOVE LEFT: *The shot requires a stiff-wristed stroke.* LEFT: *Hit the equator of the ball firmly with the flange of the club. The ball should roll toward the hole, just like a putt.*

Out of the Woods

SHAPING THE SHOTS

As a young boy, I loved practicing all day - on waste land, on the beach at Pedrena or in the rough surrounding the course, since I was hardly ever allowed to play on it. I had no choice but to improvise shots as my lies were invariably bad.

I had to work out how to hit the ball high over hills, low under branches of trees, left-to-right around tree trunks and right-to-left in cross-winds; one-handed and back-handed. There is no doubt in my mind that those long days of discovering just what was possible to do with a golf ball have helped me immeasurably in my later career. Sharing these experiences with you will, I hope, help you to cope better the next time you find yourself in dire straits.

In this chapter I will deal with all the situations, weird or wonderful, you may find your ball in during a lifetime of playing golf. Whether it be out of the woods, from below branches, or up in the bushes, some difficult lies will be a frequent feature of your golf course or your game while others will be rare occurrences. Acquaint yourself with these as well, because if you tackle them in the wrong way, you will send your scores soaring faster than a high drive into a headwind.

The High Fade

The fade is naturally a high-flying shot that comes down softly. Even from the middle of the fairway, with no trees or hazards in the way, the fade is the shot many professionals choose to hit. The soft landing makes it easier to control the ball, and to be aggressive in aiming for tight pin positions. For amateurs, the fade is simply a safer shot than the draw. A draw that gets out of control shoots left and rolls fast and farther left on landing. A fade that goes awry curves more violently than you would like, but its sidespin stops it from veering off ferociously once it hits the ground.

Remember to take more club than usual for this shot because a fade loses distance by flying from left-to-right. In the pictures on page 100, I am hitting a 3-iron when I would usually take a 4 from that range. To send the ball on a high trajectory from left to right, you shape the line of flight through the adjustments you make to your set-up. Then you swing as you would for any other shot.

On occasion you may wish to slice the ball deliberately. Just as with the draw and hook, the more left-to-right spin you want to impart on the ball, the more you will need to modify your normal swing.

For the high fade, adopt an open stance by aligning your feet to the left of the target. The club face is pointing at the pin. The ball position - well forward in your stance - together with the open stance will maximize the loft on the club and send the ball soaring high.

I find that an additional help in getting the ball up in the air for this shot is to bend my body a little to the right by dropping my right shoulder a bit more than usual. But don't put more weight on your right side. The weight should instead be evenly balanced between your feet, even though the ball is positioned forward in your stance. As a result of these adjustments to your set-up, you will come into the ball with an out-to-in shaped swing, causing the ball to fly off left-to-right.

It is very important to keep the hands slightly ahead of the ball at address, just as you would for a regular shot. Don't make the mistake of moving your hands behind the ball in a futile attempt to get the ball up in the air. Remember, in golf you hit down to get the ball up.

You may also want to grip the club a little tighter than normal with your left hand and a little more softly with your right to ensure that you maintain a firm left wrist at impact, preventing your right hand from turning the club face over. The left hand dominates the high fade.

The Low Fade

For the low fade, there are two opposing spin forces at work. The fadespin sends the ball upwards, while you try to keep it down by reducing the underspin. Consequently, the low fade requires many more alterations to your set-up position than the high fade and is far from being an easy shot.

Play the ball in the center of the stance or toward the right foot to keep its flight low. The set-up for the low fade in fact resembles a draw more than a fade, as we shall see. To shape the trajectory of the ball, however, your body must be aimed at the left of the target, just as for the high fade. In contrast to the shot we explored above, the club face must be aligned parallel to your set-up position. You will naturally swing out-to-in as intended, while you cut more sharply across the ball than you did with the high fade.

The Fade

RIGHT: *You can fade or draw the ball around the tree.* ABOVE: *This is the address position for a fade which is naturally high flying.*

The Draw

ABOVE: *Another option is to draw the ball around the obstacle. Since the low-flying draw carries and rolls farther than a normal shot, I just need a 5-iron from this distance.*

Grip down the shaft. Again, you might like to accentuate the action by gripping a bit tighter with your left hand and a little less so with your right. Your hands should remain ahead of the ball throughout the shot. The cut shot - as the low fade is sometimes called - requires a one-piece swing. So make sure that you don't break your wrists on impact and hold the club face square through the shot.

At impact you should feel as though you are cutting the club face across the ball, imparting the left-to-right spin that you want. The very nature of this action will cause you to have a restricted follow through, which is a sign of a shot well hit. Since the cut is a low-flying shot, it will run on landing, so allow for the roll when calculating where you want the ball to drop.

The Low Draw

A draw is the preferred tee shot of most professional players because it produces the maximum distance. If you have your game totally under control - and there aren't too many of us that do - then the ideal strategy is to drive the ball with a draw and hit your approach shots with a fade, since the left-to-right ball-flight of the fade will bring the ball in to land more softly. The technique that follows will stand you in good stead, even when you're playing from a perfect lie.

A hook is a more extreme version of a draw. Both veer from right-to-left and both are essentially low-flying shots. Hit off the tee or from the middle of the fairway, a hook is a draw gone bad, an unintentionally wild, curving shot that will land hot and run on fast, usually until it bounds into trouble. But if you have to get the ball to curve quickly around a tree or some other obstacle which is blocking the way to your target in close proximity, a hook is the right shot to hit. The assumption in this chapter is that you hit a hook because you wanted to, not because you've made a poor swing.

To impart the necessary sidespin on the ball, set up by dropping your right foot behind your left, thus aiming your body to the right of the target but with the club face pointing at it. This set-up will in effect close the club face in relation to your swing path, shaping your ball from right-to-left.

For greater control, go down the shaft a little with your grip. Whereas I usually place my hands for any normal shot - regardless of the club I'm using - just a touch in front of the ball at address, for this particular situation I move them distinctly forward.

The ball position should be in the center or even slightly back in the stance, depending on the length of the club you are using and the amount of curve you require. The more closed your stance and the farther back in your stance the ball, the more pronounced the right-to-left flight will be, the lower the ball will fly and the farther it will run on landing. So you should take one club less. In the photographs on page 108, I am using a 5-iron for what would normally be 4-iron range.

The closed stance will induce you to take the club back on an inside line. To encourage the inside swing path farther, make a slightly flatter swing than you normally would. If you are one of those players who likes to have a specific swing though, think about rotating your hands through the ball as you come into it - you have to turn your right hand over the left as you take them through impact. The fact that the right hand crosses over the left to apply the drawspin to the ball will inevitably lead you into a full follow through. However, because of the flatter swing plane, your shoulders will turn lower than usual. By then, the ball should be nicely on its way.

The High Draw

The very notion of this shot is a contradiction in terms. The natural flight of a draw is low, as the right-to-left spin pulls the ball down. The most effective way to hit a higher draw is simply to take a more lofted club. That is obvious and therefore often the best advice. If the distance would normally require you to take a 5-iron and you have a tree to go over and around, the best solution may well be to choose the 7 instead.

Sometimes you want to get the best of both worlds - a high trajectory and distance. I particularly remember one occasion when I needed just that, at the first hole in the second round of the 1988 Masters at Augusta. I had pulled my drive into the trees to the left of the fairway and needed a high ball to escape the overhanging branches and a draw to land on the green. Golf strokes don't always work out as you hope, but let me tell you how I saved my par.

The technique required for such a shot is similar to the one employed for the regular draw. To shape the flight of the ball from right-to-left, set up with a closed stance pointing to the right of the target and with the club face squared to it. The club face will effectively be closed at impact as a consequence. Your swing path will again follow an inside line, encouraged by the closed stance.

The Low Fade

OVERLEAF, TOP: *Choke down on the club for better control since the fade is a high shot. Take an open stance with the clubhead pointing at your target but your feet aligned to the left of it. Play the ball backward in your stance.* BOTTOM: *You want to make an out-to-in shaped swing, sending the ball on a left-to-right flight. Grip a little more firmly than normal with your left hand and a little more softly with the right.* PAGE 105, TOP: *This post impact shot of the low fade shows how the left side is dominant. My open set-up has led to an out-to-in attack on the ball, with the hands staying ahead of the ball throughout the swing.* BOTTOM: *This shot has a one-piece swing. You do not break your wrists through impact but instead hold the club face open through the shot. The follow through is restricted. You can also see here that I have choked down on the grip to play this shot.*

The ball must be placed forward in your stance, the extent to which depending on the club you are using and the amount of curve you hope to put on the ball. The ball position will help you to get the ball to rise quickly. Your hands should be ahead of the ball at address, but you must remember to rotate them through the ball on the downswing, crossing your right hand over the left through impact to apply the drawspin to the ball. You strike the ball with your body weight settled behind it, and you should finish your swing higher than you would when playing a low draw shot.

The Punch

The first mistake many amateurs make when trying to punch the ball low is to hit it too hard. If the strike is absolutely perfect, they might get away with it, but usually contact is far from ideal, and that puts spin on the shot when they least want it. Too much spin will either send the ball up in the air or curving to the left or right, sacrificing both distance and direction.

Play the ball back in your stance, just inside the right heel. This delofts the club and establishes the angle at which you want the club face to hit the ball on the way back down. A word of warning, though. Don't use anything less lofted than a 5-iron for this shot. If you attempt the punch shot with your 3-iron, for example, the delofted club face will resemble that of a 1-iron, and how good are you with that club?

Go down the grip a bit for improved feel and position your weight more on the left side than usual. These adjustments not only help you keep the ball low but also restrict your backswing so that you can come down with a steep, sharp stabbing action and deliver the clubhead with accuracy into the ball.

The punch demands very little hand action. The hands should stay ahead of the clubhead throughout the swing. Maintain a firm left side throughout, as pre-set by your weight distribution at address. The abbreviated backswing and that firm left side will lead to a shortened follow through. You ought to feel as though you are chasing the ball off to its destination, keeping the clubhead low to the ground as it goes on its way.

The Shot from Tree Roots

When your ball has come to nestle among the roots of a tree, you may not have a choice address position - if the ball is playable at all. However, as long as you can find a spot where you can reasonably stand and you can get the club to the ball, then you should take the opportunity to play the shot.

Open the club face well as you need as much loft as you can get on the ball. Choke down on the grip to increase your control over the club. The swing has to be necessarily steep so that you can deliver the club face to the ball. If you are playing right next to the tree trunk, as I do in the photographs on page 110, your backswing will be restricted and you won't be able to make a body turn at all. The right hand will then dominate this shot, since it is the only part of your body with which you will be able to generate any power from behind the tree.

The proximity of the tree roots will severely curtail your follow through, but resist the temptation to look up too early to see where the ball has gone. Rather, keep your eyes on the ball so that you don't damage your clubhead or your hands by striking the roots too solidly. If you foresee any danger to your equipment or - more important - to yourself, take a one-shot penalty for an unplayable lie and drop away from the tree. There is always another round tomorrow.

The Covered Lie

You've encountered this sort of situation, I'm sure, many more times than you care to remember, and although I'm smiling in the pictures on page 116, this lie is no laughing matter. But there is also no need to panic. You can still make an effective swing at the ball.

Although you can see the ball, you can't address it properly. Don't try to touch any part of the brambles, shrub, bush, heather or whatever you're in. If you do, the chances are that you will cause the ball to move, which, in turn, will cost you a one-stroke penalty. Furthermore, if you attempt to start your swing with the club right behind the ball, the odds are that the clubhead will snag on the takeaway and probably ruin the shot right from the outset.

The best strategy to escape from a covered lie is to get back into play in the safest possible manner. You need a lot of loft to cut through the weeds to your ball. So don't use anything with less loft than an 8-iron.

Play the ball off your right foot to pick it as cleanly as possible off the ground. You also need to choke down on the grip for a better feel for the movement of the clubhead. Make as full and as normal a swing as you possibly can. On the downswing, hit the ball hard. The club is almost bound to get caught up in the shrubs, and you need to strike down at the ball with power and energy in order to propel it back to the fairway. If you let the bushes distract you and decelerate your swing, you will almost

The Low Draw

RIGHT: *To play the draw, close the club face at address. Go down the shaft a little bit with your grip, and close your stance by dropping your right foot behind your left. The ball position should be in the center of your stance or even farther backward, and your hands should remain ahead of the ball. Aim right of the target.*
BELOW RIGHT: *Take the club back on an inside line and make a flatter swing than normal. You can see here how flat my right shoulder is on the takeaway.* BOTTOM RIGHT: *Through impact, rotate your hands through the ball, the right hand coming over the left. You can see that leads to a flatter finish than usual, but nevertheless uninhibited.*

The High Draw

LEFT: *To hit a high draw, the set-up is similar to that for the regular draw. But you can see that my body is more behind the ball.* BELOW LEFT: *My shoulders are slightly higher through the swing, which will lead to a higher finish than for a normal draw.* BOTTOM LEFT: *Notice that my right hand is turning over the left.*

certainly leave the ball in the lush wilderness or knock it scrambling into a worse place.

The Perched Lie

Here we are again deep in the woodworks, with the ball hanging about two feet above the ground in the twigs of a bush. In other words, the ball nestles severely above your feet and you have to apply a similar technique to the one we discussed for the uneven lie.

Use a club with as little loft as you feel confident with - say, a 4-iron - whenever you find your ball suspended mid-air. Once the club hits the shrubbery on the downswing, the twigs will twist the club face open and your 4-iron will effectively have the loft of a 6-iron. For this reason, you won't want to use anything as short as a wedge here.

In the photographs on pages 118 and 119, you will notice how I have choked down on the grip because the ball is now much closer to the clubhead than on level ground. Be careful at address not to touch the foliage the ball is resting on so that you don't dislodge the ball unintentionally. Take the club away on the same level on which the ball is lying without bending your wrists too early or trying to jerk up the club to a more upright swing position.

For the perched lie, your swing plane needs to be very flat, with the club rotating around your waist. Your backswing will be naturally restricted by the foliage around you, but you should make a three-quarter turn if you can at all.

Keep your hands firm and steady through impact despite the leaves and twigs in the way of the clubhead. The ball will fly off to the left on a low trajectory with a lot of roll on landing. Pick your aim carefully.

The Restricted Swing

When the branches obstruct your backswing and follow through, you need to swing on a very flat plane to be able to swing at all. The shot is therefore dominated by the hand action. As a rule of thumb, don't choose anything more lofted than an 8-iron and nothing less lofted than a 5-iron. You don't want to scuff the ball along the ground with a longer club than you can handle or still find yourself in the woods with too lofted a club.

The Shot from Tree Roots

OPPOSITE, LEFT AND BELOW FAR LEFT: *When trying to play out from tree roots, you should have the club face well open at address. Choke down on the grip for more control.* BELOW CENTER LEFT: *There is no body turn here. It is a right-hand dominated shot, and the tree roots will severely restrict your follow through.* BELOW LEFT: *Resist the temptation to look up too early to see where the ball has gone.*

The Right-Handed
Toe Shot

ABOVE: *The tree roots here prevent a proper address with the sweet spot of the club face.* RIGHT: *Address that ball off the toe of the club, using whatever club you feel comfortable with.* OPPOSITE: *Stand open, with a narrow stance. Grip well down the shaft and swing the club away with your hands and arms.* OVERLEAF: *Concentrate on making clean contact with the ball and driving it forwards. Keep your head down through the shot until the ball is on its way.* PAGE 115: *This is all the follow through you need.*

The Covered Lie

RIGHT: *Do not touch any part of the branches at address. If you do, you may cause the ball to move, which will cost you a one-shot penalty.* BELOW RIGHT: *Play the ball off a point opposite your right foot and choke down on the grip. Then hit the ball as hard as you can.* BOTTOM RIGHT: *The club is bound to get caught up in the branches, but that does not matter once the ball has gone.*

You need to swing on an extremely flat plane, basically rotating the club with your hands around your body. To give this flat swing a proper base, widen your stance significantly, as I have done in the photographs on pages 120, 122 and 124 . Bend your knees a lot more than you normally would. Note that the butt-end of the club is at the same height as my (lower) right knee, a factor that encourages the ball to come out low under the branches. Set up with a closed stance to farther ensure a low trajectory of the ball for this shot.

You will see that I have not cocked my wrists too quickly. If I did, the clubhead would get caught up in the branches. For a shot that has little body movement, the amount of wrist cock here is minimal.

The power comes from the hand action through the ball. The swing is like a vigorous swish, with the right hand turning over the left through impact, just as it does when you try to draw or hook the ball. This hand action again assists in producing a low trajectory and propels the ball for quite a distance. With practice you can learn to punt the ball anything up to 70 or 80 yards with a restricted swing.

The Shot on the Knees

The shot from a kneeling position is an exaggerated version of the shot we have just studied. Although you may doubt your chances of successfully playing what most resembles a trick shot, a mixture of ingenuity and common sense can save you from a penalty drop. This shot will literally bring you to your knees, but it doesn't have to ruin your round.

The best club for the shot on your knees is often the 6-iron. Since you need to keep the ball low, a more lofted club will usually be too risky to take, and if you try to hit anything longer, you might find it very hard to get the ball airborne at all.

Take a stance on your knees that makes you feel comfortable. From this address position you have no choice but to swing on a very shallow plane, which will also help you to keep the club below the level of the branches around you. The swing is mostly a turning motion around your torso. The shaft of the club is low to the ground and the club face is pointing upward as much as forward.

You need to shorten the club slightly because of your stance. But to give yourself greater control over the club from this awkward position, you

The Perched Lie

OVERLEAF, LEFT: *Take a club with little loft and choke down on the grip for better control.*
RIGHT: *As before, hit the ball hard, maintaining good balance and keeping your head steady.* PAGE 119: *The club has got caught in the shrubs, but once again the ball is on its way.*

PRECEDING PAGES :
120 AND 121: *In this*
situation, you need to
make a very flat swing, so
first of all widen your
stance. Bend your knees
much more than you
normally would, and
draw your right foot
behind your left. The
butt-end of the club is at
about the same height as
my right knee, which will
encourage the ball to
come out low, under the
branches. PAGES 122
AND 123: *Don't cock*
your wrists too quickly
otherwise the clubhead
gets ensnared by the
branches. PAGES 124
AND 125: *The power*
comes from the hands as
they swish vigorously
through the ball, the right
hand turning over the left
both to generate power
and to keep the ball low.

probably want to grip even farther down the shaft, as I have done in the photographs on page 127.

Since this shot is purely dependent on the hand action, you don't need to cock your wrists much, so that the clubhead can be kept below the branches. Into impact, your arms should feel as if they are about to sweep the ball off the ground. Don't be too ambitious with this shot. Get the ball out as far as you can by all means, but make sure you do get it out.

One final tip. As I have done when I played this shot for the photographs, you might want to put on your waterproof trousers if the ground is at all damp. But be careful about what measures you take to protect your clothing. You will perhaps recall the case of the former Masters champion, Craig Stadler, who was once disqualified from a tournament for putting a towel under his knees to play this shot. Compared to that, a one-shot penalty would have been a price worth paying. With a little work on unorthodox shots like this, you needn't suffer either fate.

The Single-Handed Shot

The single-handed shot is played with your right hand if you are right-handed and with your left if you are not. This shotmaking technique comes in handy when you cannot face in the direction you want to send the ball. In the illustrations overleaf you can see that I would have comparatively little trouble in hitting the ball normally if I were left-handed. Since I'm not, I have to hit the ball backward.

Take your stance with your back facing the target. I like to stand a normal distance away from the ball, much as I would for any routine shot, but with an open stance (assuming I was trying to hit the ball forward). The ball is placed opposite my right foot.

Choke down on the grip for more control. This is a hard shot to control, and you need to be confident about hitting it before you attempt it in competitive play. Even then, get a feel for how to play the shot. Take a few practice swings to ingrain the right thoughts and movements into your mind and body.

Allow the club to hang straight down from your grip. Because you are standing with your back to the target, you will not be able to ground the club as you would for an orthodox shot, so the hitting area of the club face is substantially reduced. Therefore don't attempt to achieve any significant distance with this shot. I suggest you play it with an 8-iron, although the lie

The Shot on the Knees

ABOVE LEFT: *Take a stance that feels comfortable. Your swing is going to be very flat, which you want in order to keep the club below the level of the branches. Note how far down the grip I have gone.*

ABOVE: *The swing is mostly a turning motion around your torso.*

LEFT: *There is little wrist cock with this shot. Your arms should feel as if they are going to sweep the ball off the ground.*

BELOW LEFT: *Do not be too ambitious from this situation, but as you can see, it is possible to get the ball airborne!*

The Single-Handed Shot

RIGHT: *Take your stance with your back facing the target at a normal distance from the ball, with an open stance. The ball is played off a spot opposite the right foot. Choke well down on the grip for more control. Allow the club to hang straight down from your grip.* BELOW RIGHT: *Take the club straight up on the takeaway and then straight back down in a pendulum motion.* BELOW FAR RIGHT: *The hitting area of the club face is substantially reduced for this shot, so do not attempt to gain any great distance with it.*

may force you to select a shorter club. Take the club straight up on the takeaway and then straight back down in a pendulum motion.

You will be aware that you should always keep your eye on the ball when playing golf. It may sound contradictory to emphasize this for the single-handed shot, but since the margin for error in this case is very small, it is even more important that you keep your head steady in this situation than in all others. Among all the tricky shots in this book, this may be the easiest with which to miss the ball entirely, and if you have an air shot, not only will you feel embarrassed, you will still have to play the shot again.

As nerve-racking as this shot is, I have played it under the gun. In the final of the 1981 World Match Play Championship at Wentworth, I was all-square on the 12th tee of the afternoon round against Ben Crenshaw. I then drove into the woods, of which there are plenty on the West Course, and the only way to get back on to the fairway in one shot was to hit the ball one-handed. I duly got the ball out, knocked my third shot on to the green, and made my par five.

The bad news was that Ben made a birdie four, but in the end I won the match on the last green.

The Left-Handed Shot

You will have to be in fairly dire straits to attempt this shot, but as golf is hardly fair, a knowledge of the two variations of the left-handed shot may come in handy one day. The shot can be played by striking the ball either with the toe of the club or with the back of the clubhead if you are using blade irons. The technique in both cases is essentially the same. However, you want to use a lofted club for the toe shot, to send the ball as far upward as possible and to increase your margin of error, whereas for the variation played off the back of the blade, you need to pick a longer club for exactly the same reasons.

Set up to the ball as you would for a routine right-handed shot in reverse. Take an orthodox left-handed grip, with your left hand below the right. Grip well down the shaft for more control. Set up with a narrow, open stance to make clean contact with the ball. If you are going to hit the ball with the toe of the club, have the toe resting on the ground. If you are going to strike it with the back of the club, address the ball with the club grounded as normal - except that now the back of the club - always provided that you are playing with blades - is facing the ball!

In both cases, you set up with the ball off your left heel in order to promote the downward strike you need to help get the ball up into the air. When you take aim, allow for the tendency of the ball to shoot quite sharply to the left when struck with the back of a club. Off the toe, the shape of the shot will depend on the quality of the contact. Align your body square to the target.

Take a few more practice swings than usual to familiarize yourself with the sensation of swinging left-handedly. Then swing as normally as you can. The ball is hit with a stiff-wristed blow, the back of your right hand facing the target as you make contact with the ball.

As with the single-handed shot, it is especially important to keep your head steady and your eye on the ball when attempting to play left handedly. You are doing something out of the ordinary and are therefore likely to be tempted to look up too early to see where the ball has gone. Don't.

I have played left-handed shots in tournaments more often than I care to remember, and more often than I can recall. One occasion, however, has stayed in my mind.

At the Chunichi Crowns tournament in Japan, my ball had landed 150 yards from the green, close to an out-of-bounds fence on the left which meant I couldn't play an orthodox shot. When my caddie, Billy Foster, realized what I was going to attempt, he suggested that I laid up. But sometimes you feel confident about pulling off a highly risky shot, and this was just such an occasion.

I took out my 8-iron and played the left-handed shot with the toe of the club. It worked, and I hit the ball almost on to the green.

The Left-Handed Shot off the Back

ABOVE: *Playing the ball left-handed with the back of the club, set up as for a normal shot - just with everything in reverse. Ground the club with the back of the club facing the ball.* OPPOSITE, ABOVE FAR LEFT: *Play the ball off your left heel to help get it airborne.* ABOVE LEFT: *Swing as normally as you can.* FAR LEFT: *Hit the ball with a stiff-wristed blow, the back of your right hand facing toward the target.* LEFT: *The ball is likely to shoot sharply to the left.*

The Left-Handed Shot off the Toe

RIGHT: *To play the shot left-handed off the toe of the club, address the ball with the toe resting on the ground. Try to make as normal a swing as you can, and concentrate on keeping your head still and maintaining your balance through the shot. This is tough enough to execute well as it is!*

Awkward Spots

ALONG THE FAIRWAY

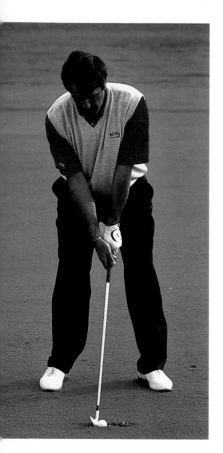

We may be out of the woods, but we are by no means out of trouble. On the golf course, you can find yourself frequently in awkward spots that require you to play unfamiliar shots. If you are not so unfortunate as to encounter the situations I will deal with in this chapter all during one round, you will probably find yourself in at least one of them every time you go out to play.

The Long Shot from a Divot

A divot causes more worries for the average club golfer than need be the case. It is simply a matter of knowing your capabilities and using common sense. Above all, leave your ambitions in the clubhouse.

When you are facing a long shot on to the green from a divot, analyze the situation. You may have some 200 yards to go, but don't let that tempt you into reaching for your 3-wood. A perfect strike with that wood is something you probably only achieve in one out of ten attempts at best. Anything less, however, will cause the ball to flop out of the hole in the ground and tumble forward a mere 30 or 40 yards toward the flag. When that happens, you will still need a long iron to get home. It is therefore better to take a 5-iron and leave yourself with nothing more than a wedge into the green.

Open the club face more than usual to get at the ball better. Play the ball a little farther back in your stance than normal, with your weight appreciably more on the left side than on the right in order to pick the ball cleanly off the ground. For the same purpose, take a steeper swing than you normally would by cocking your wrists early in the backswing.

To avoid hitting the ground heavily and propelling the ball nowhere at all, swing on an out-to-in line, cutting across the ball to hit it clean. Your swing path and the open club face will cause the ball to spin off to the right, so you should aim left of your intended target. The ball will cut back on line.

The ball position back in your stance results in a lower trajectory than you would normally get and a lot of roll on landing. So don't try and attack a tight pin position or float the ball in over a greenside bunker. Aim for an area which gives the ball room to run on safely.

The Long Shot from a Divot

ABOVE: *When you have to play a full-shot from a divot, take nothing more than a 5-iron. Open the club face and play the ball a little farther back in your stance to promote a steeper swing.* OPPOSITE, ABOVE RIGHT: *Cock your wrists early and make a full turn.* ABOVE FAR RIGHT: *Swing on an out-to-in path, cutting across the ball.* RIGHT: *The ball flies low.* PRECEDING PAGES: *A shot gone awry hit the tree first and me second.*

The Short Shot from a Divot

ABOVE: *A ball in a divot right in front of the green is not a pleasant sight at the end of a great shot.* RIGHT: *Play the ball off your back foot and choke down on the grip. The lie will result in a low trajectory of the ball. Aim a little left of the flag and open the club face.* ABOVE FAR RIGHT: *Cock your wrists early, and swing on an outside path.* RIGHT: *On the steep downswing, you want to make contact with the ground just before the ball.* FAR RIGHT: *Hold the club face square through impact. Do not let your right hand roll over the left.*

The Short Shot from a Divot

The short shot from a divot resembles an explosion shot from a bunker. Open the club face to get to the ball and aim a little left of the flag to compensate for the sidespin you will impart on the ball. Choke down on the grip for more control over the clubhead. Cock the wrists early to set up for a steep backswing and swing on an outside plane to propel the ball quickly out of the divot and ensure that you don't end up pushing it deeper in.

Play the ball off your right foot to impart a steep, downward blow on the ball. To offset the low trajectory resulting from this ball position, play the short shot from the divot with a wedge, but don't expect to get the ball up as quickly as usual. Bear the low flight pattern in mind, especially if you have to carry a hazard before the green.

Coming down, make firm contact with the ground and the ball at the same time, rather than try to hit the ball cleanly. This is a sharply descending blow and you need to hit down harder than you normally would for a shot of this distance. Anything too tentative and as sure as misery follows a shank, you will still be short of the green, or else miles over it. Hold the club face square through impact and don't let your right hand roll over your left.

If you adjust your swing accordingly and let the loft of the club do the rest of the work for you, you needn't feel that fate has dealt you a harsh blow the next time your ball ends up in a divot. Instead, it will be an opportunity for you to demonstrate another facet of your game.

The Hardpan Lie

Now I'll wager that this is a shot you've had to play quite a bit. Despite the amount of grass on a golf course, it is amazing how often your ball can come to rest on an old road or path, and there is no relief available in the form of a free drop. Although the ground you are playing from is considerably firmer than the turf, the shot itself need not be that hard.

From a hardpan lie, the ball will come out lower than after a shot struck with the same club from the fairway because you will catch the ball thinner than you would from a fairway lie. Since it is difficult to propel the ball into the air from a hardpan lie, make sure that you take a more lofted club than you normally would for the same distance, particularly if there is a tree or bush on the line you intend to take.

In their attempts to get the ball airborne, I see many amateur golfers in pro-ams trying to scoop the ball off the ground, inevitably leading to their topping the shot. Their anxiety over the fact that the ground is hard causes them to commit the very mistake that they are so desperate to avoid.

To compensate for the hardpan lie, stand a little taller at address than you normally would by having your feet a little closer together than usual. The ball should be played back in the stance, toward the right foot so that you can pick the ball cleanly off the ground. Hold your hands ahead of the ball throughout the swing for the same purpose. On the downswing, be sure to keep your left wrist firm through impact. If you don't, you will probably suffer that dreaded, feeble, scoop shot. For a short shot from the hardpan lie, use a pitching wedge rather than a sand wedge as it has less bounce.

If the ball is sitting down a bit in the hardpan lie, perhaps in a shallow depression, make your swing just a little more upright to make sure that you catch the ball before the ground and play the ball even more off your back foot.

I played exactly this same shot during the 1992 Dubai Desert Classic, my 50th career victory on the PGA European Tour. In the opening round, I found my ball on the yellow ground swept clean of sand by the winds. The wind was blowing against me and I needed a 4-iron to get home. I struck the shot in the same manner I have just described, and not only saved my par but made a birdie. Just as well, really. I only won the tournament after a playoff with Ronan Rafferty.

The Powdery Lie

If you find your ball in sandy waste, on ground covered with pine needles, or in the collection of twigs and leaves you see here, clear away as much of the debris as you can, to make your powdery lie less powdery.

In doing this you have to be very careful not to move the ball, which would lead to you incurring a penalty. Under Rule 18-2, Clause c, "if the ball moves after any loose impediment, lying within a club-length of it has been touched by the player, his partner or either of their caddies…the player shall be deemed to have moved the ball and shall incur a penalty stroke."

Be wary of moving any twig that might cause another one to move, which ultimately may dislodge the ball itself. That will make you one stroke worse off, and you haven't even tried to hit the ball yet. (If this happens to you,

The Hardpan Lie

OPPOSITE, ABOVE FAR LEFT: *Since it is harder to get the ball into the air from hardpan, take a more lofted club than normal. Stand a little taller at address than you ordinarily would, with your feet a little closer together. The ball should be played back in the stance, well toward the right foot.* ABOVE CENTER LEFT: *You are going to try to pick the ball up cleanly off the ground, but your swing should feel normal.* LEFT: *Keep your left wrist firm through impact and your hands ahead of the ball throughout.* ABOVE: *Complete your follow through.*

make sure you replace the ball where it was before playing your shot, or you will incur a farther penalty shot.)

This process can be quite painstaking. I clearly remember watching José María Olazábal patiently clearing pine needles and cones from around his ball after his drive had missed the 13th fairway in the final round of the 1994 Masters, which he went on to win. You don't want to take forever doing this, but don't rush to the extent that you cost yourself an extra shot.

If you have been fortunate in your attempts to improve your lie in this manner, then the shot is played like any other. But if the lie is still not so good, and there is still a lot of debris around the ball, make a few adjustments to your ordinary swing.

Hover the clubhead behind the ball at address rather than ground it. This might be your preferred strategy at all times, as it is for Jack Nicklaus, but in any case, do it here. This is also another safeguard to stop you from causing the ball to move unnecessarily - and expensively!

From this type of lie, you want to hit the ball with a steeply descending blow so as to reduce the risk of the clubhead getting entangled in the loose impediments before impact. To help you do this, play the ball off your right foot, keep your hands ahead of the ball throughout the swing, and keep most of your weight on your left side. The circumstances of the lie and your angle of attack into the ball will tend to deloft the club you use, so allow for that by taking a more lofted club than you would normally use for a shot of the distance you have.

The Shot over a Hazard

Many club golfers get anxious about a shot like this well before they reach their ball. They are already thinking that if they mess it up, they will be in the bunker, water or whatever hazard is in front of them. Most professionals, on the other hand, don't notice those things. They just see the green and the flag - that is, where they want the ball to go, not where they don't.

Another mistake amateurs are guilty of - assuming they don't fall prey to the water - is the fact that they seldom get to the flag on any hole with their shot to the green. The next time you play, go back over your round afterward and count the number of times your approach to the green, from whatever distance, finished past the hole rather than fell short of it. Not often, I bet, allowing that on most holes, there is more trouble short than there is long.

With the longer clubs, this error largely occurs because many golfers do not take enough club. They seem to think that they will either hit the ball farther than they actually do, or else they assume they are about to hit the shot of their career.

If you don't want to leave the ball short of the hole, imagine that you are aiming at the top of the flag, not at the bottom. Having that sort of focus will also take your mind off the water. You shouldn't think about the water.

The shot documented in the photographs on pages 144 and 145 is a short shot with a pitching wedge or a sand wedge, whichever you prefer, and not even a full one at that. The lie is an average rough lie in long grass, not better or worse than any you may find on a typical course.

Set up with an open stance with the ball in the center and make sure that your hands are ahead of the ball at address so you can hit down to get the ball up in the air. Choke down on the grip a little, as I have done for this shot, so that you can hit the ball harder and with a fuller swing, leading to a fuller follow through, rather than making a shorter swing or - often a worse mistake - trying to hit a softer shot. For amateur golfers especially, it is often best to hit a full shot rather than try to finesse one. And that's especially true if you are still bothered about that water!

Make sure you stay down through impact. If you look up too quickly, you might indeed bring the water into the game. Let the club do the work of getting the ball up in the air and carrying it to the flag. It's the ball that you want to get over the water, not your body. Try to imagine that the shaft of the club is an extension of your left arm.

In the 1995 Ryder Cup singles against Tom Lehman at Oak Hill, I had lost the opening hole. The 2nd hole is a shortish par four, and Tom was on the green in two strokes, some ten feet from the cup. I lay two some 20 yards from the flag, with a bunker about halfway to the stick and not much green to work with thereafter. I knew the shot was good as soon as I hit it, but it turned out even better than I thought and the ball popped into the cup. When Lehman missed his putt, we were level. Unfortunately, my long game was so ragged that day, and Tom's was so good, that I still lost the match on the 15th green. But on that day, with Europe eventually winning a nerve-jangling tournament, I felt like a winner anyway.

The Powdery Lie

OPPOSITE, ABOVE LEFT: A powdery lie. LEFT: *Try to clear away as much of the debris as you safely can.* BELOW LEFT: *This is the result of our little gardening session - a normally playable ball.* TOP: *Be very careful when you touch a leaf or twig.* ABOVE: *Keep your hands off if the ball is nestling on thick debris which - once moved - may dislodge the ball in turn.*

The Shot over a Hazard

RIGHT: *Set up with the ball in the center of your stance and your hands ahead of it. Choke down on the grip a little, as I have done here, so that you can hit the ball with an almost full swing.* BELOW RIGHT: *I am standing a little bit open to help get the ball up into the air.* FAR RIGHT: *The length of the swing depends on the distance your ball needs to carry. Imagine that the shaft of the club is like an extension of your left arm.* OPPOSITE: *Make sure you stay down through impact, make a confident strike at the ball, and let the club do the work of getting the ball over the water and up to the flag.*

The Shot out of Water

After your ball disappears with a big splash in the pond, the most sensible strategy may well be to declare the ball unplayable and take a drop under penalty. Under certain circumstances, however, it may be worth evaluating the situation in more detail.

Don't play out of water unless at least a quarter of the ball is showing above the surface. Otherwise, take the drop for a simple reason: when light penetrates the surface of water, it refracts at an angle. In other words, when you think you see your ball under water you actually see only a reflection of it – the ball doesn't lie where you think it does. As if you didn't already have enough problems to contend with!

Should you attempt to play the shot, make sure that you can take a firm-footed stance. This shot is hard enough without worrying about falling into the water yourself. The next move is a sartorial one: put on your waterproofs! You will need them. Since water is a designated hazard, just as in a bunker, you cannot ground the club - or in this case, attempt to drown it. In other words, you must not touch the surface of the water prior to executing the shot.

The technique for this shot is similar to playing from under an overhanging lip of a bunker, although from water, you may prefer to use your pitching wedge rather than the sand wedge because its sharper leading edge comes more handy for slashing through the water.

At address, open the club face slightly, position the ball slightly right of center in your stance, and take the club back with a steep backswing, cocking your wrists fully and early. The contact here is with the ground under the water, not with the ball itself. Hit down very hard just behind the ball, just as you would to play an explosion shot from the sand. The hands stay ahead of the ball all the way, and you should stay down on the shot through impact. Resist the temptation to look up too early to assess the results of your handiwork. The subsequent splash is why you need your waterproofs. As with a shot from the sand, the ball should fly out softly.

Playing out of a water hazard is a risky shot. So that you are aware of all possible options, including the rules governing how to take a drop from water, which in themselves differ depending on the type of water hazard you are in, you should read Rule 26 of the Rules of Golf, which can be obtained free from your club.

The Shot out of Water

ABOVE: *Do not attempt to play a shot out of water unless at least a quarter of the ball is showing above the surface.* OPPOSITE, RIGHT: *Get those waterproofs on!* ABOVE FAR RIGHT: *Make sure you can take a firm-footed stance.* FAR RIGHT: *Open the club face slightly and have the ball a little back in your stance.* BELOW FAR RIGHT: *Take the club back with a steep backswing, cocking your wrists fully and early.* OVERLEAF: *Hit down very hard just behind the ball, as you would to play an explosion shot from a bunker.* PAGE 149: *You can see that my hands have stayed ahead of the clubhead. As with a shot from sand, the ball should fly out softly.*

Facing the Elements

WEATHER ARITHMETICS

Given a choice, all golfers would prefer to play in calm conditions rather than in a stiff wind, which makes it harder to swing well and to judge yardages. But none of us can control the weather. When the wind blows, regard it as a challenge to be relished. If you confront adverse weather with that attitude, it need not wreck your timing and tempo. If you are playing a friendly round, you can look upon it as an opportunity to further your shotmaking skills. If you are playing in a competition, remember that the wind is the same for everyone, and that the player who tackles it with the most positive attitude is likely to be the one who handles it best.

At the British Open Championship each July, we generally encounter windy conditions, but that is as it should be. The great links of the British Isles were designed with the assumption that the wind would blow. The elements are an integral part of the golfing examination. Growing up as I did in the coastal town of Pedrena, I soon got used to the fact that still days were the exception, not the rule. You are probably aware that the Bay of Santander is not renowned for its calm weather.

When the wind is up, expect your scores to go up as well. Don't be dismayed by the results. If you normally expect to shoot an 80, then on a windy day that might become an 85, or even a 90. Accept that fact, because after all, it is the same for everyone. Many times in my career I have shot a 72 in bad weather that I would regard as markedly superior to the 65 that I produced the day before when the sun was out and the flags were hanging motionless on their sticks.

If you take that attitude to the golf course on the next windy day you get out there, you might be pleasantly surprised by how well you score. Don't think "I'll never be able to play in this weather", because then you won't. Your defeatist mentality will become a self-fulfilling prophecy. Instead, adjust your personal par for the day. Aim to shoot that 85, or the 90, and base your game plan for each hole on that premise. That way, you might find you will end up closer to 80 after all, and you will feel more positive and confident than you would have had you gone out already beaten.

You need to adjust your strategy to the weather. The wind you are playing in is bound to have a bearing on which hazards are in play. Into the wind, you might have problems carrying a pond that on a calm day you could clear with ease. With a tailwind, those fearsome traps some 250 yards out might now be within reach of your driver. With a cross-wind, a remote area that's out-of-bounds might suddenly be a real threat. Take those factors into account before you play your shot.

The Shot into the Wind

Contrary to what you might think, when you are playing into a wind, the last thing you should do is try to hit the cover off the ball. All spin is exaggerated when the ball flies into a headwind, so you want to hit it more easily and softly, to reduce backspin and prevent it from ballooning. If you try to hit the ball hard in strong wind or swing too quickly, you can easily be blown off balance and ruin your shot.

To offset the effect of the headwind, take more club. The stronger the wind, the longer the club you need to choose. For a normal 7-iron distance, you may well have to take a 4-iron into the breeze. Most amateurs underestimate the strength of the wind, or overestimate their own capabilities. Granted, it isn't easy to make yourself hit a 4-iron when your yardage chart tells you the distance to the flag is less than 140 yards. But I bet you don't hit the ball over the green frequently when the wind is against you.

Choke down on the grip a bit. Doing this will enhance your feel for the shot and help to promote a lower-flying shot. Make sure your hands stay ahead of the ball throughout the swing and put the majority of your weight on your left side. These two moves will also keep the ball down.

The fact that your weight is concentrated on your left side will naturally restrict the length of the swing. A compact swing, maybe of three-quarter length, is the safest strategy under the circumstances, to keep the movement smooth and rhythmical while the wind is pulling at you. You might also want to widen your stance to give yourself a greater sense of balance when you are hitting into a particularly strong wind.

I place my ball in its usual position in my stance. If the ball is played well back in the stance, as many people advocate, you will impart too much backspin on the ball. This ball position often leads to a feeble shot that balloons into the air, not a powerful blow that bores under the wind.

Coming down, concentrate on keeping the grip end of the club ahead of the club face. This should help you to keep the ball under the wind. The feeling you should have through impact is that of keeping the clubhead low

The Shot into the Wind

ABOVE: *Choke down on the grip to improve your feel for the clubhead. Concentrate your weight on your left side.* ABOVE RIGHT: *Take the club away around your body on a shallow swing plane.* ABOVE FAR RIGHT: *Keep the swing rhythmical and smooth.* RIGHT: *Make sure your hands stay ahead of the ball throughout the swing.* FAR RIGHT: *Keep the clubhead low to the ground, chasing the ball away as you finish with a balanced follow through.*

to the ground and chasing the ball off on a low trajectory as you go into your follow through. This is basically a one-piece action; there is not too much movement of the hands or the wrists.

For the tee shot into the wind, you should tee-up the ball a little lower than normal to encourage it to fly lower. Be especially careful with regard to your footing. The wind will be trying to push you backward, and because a swing with the driver creates the biggest arc, you will be more vulnerable to being blown off balance. Remember, swing easy.

A headwind has one big advantage, though. It lends itself perfectly for a practice session. If you have a tendency to hook or slice the ball, the wind will exaggerate those faults, and you can work on remedying them until the ball flies straight. If you can hit the ball straight into a wind, you will know that your game is going well

The Downwind Shot

When you kick a football with your right foot, the right side of your body will naturally fall below your left as you kick it, and your weight should stay behind the ball after impact. The same applies to the golf shot, especially when you are playing downwind.

With the wind at your back, you sometimes feel that you can do no wrong. Your drive will fly for miles; you can hit a distant green with a dazzling long-iron shot if you play it correctly. In your excitement at the chance to hit a screamer, don't lose sight of what you have to do. There are few feelings in golf more demoralizing than being all set up for a great shot and then duffing it completely.

With the wind at your back, you want to get the ball up into the air in order to capitalize on the elements. Therefore, concentrate your weight on your right side at address. Place the ball forward in your stance, opposite your left heel, or even farther forward to promote a better use of your hands in the hitting area.

The swing itself should be upright, so that the ball is propelled upward. Pick the club up comparatively steeply on the backswing which will lead you to attack the ball with a correspondingly steep downswing. Through impact, you should feel that your right side is pushing under your left. As with the football, try to stay behind the ball for as long as possible until your high finish.

The Downwind Shot

OPPOSITE: *Your weight should be primarily on your right side, and your swing more upright than normal. Through impact, feel that your right side is pushing under your left. The high finish you see here is how you should conclude your swing, too.*

The Shot in a Right-To-Left Wind

OVERLEAF, LEFT TO RIGHT, TOP TO BOTTOM: *To hit the ball left-to-right, open your stance, with the ball well back in it, and choke down on the grip. Take more club than usual from this distance, and use only a three-quarter swing. On your takeaway, you should feel as though you are separating your hands from your body. Feel as though you are chopping across the ball. Your left hand controls the shot, so grip a little more firmly than normal with that hand. Don't let the clubhead get ahead of your hands. Beyond impact, see how my left side dominates the follow through position.*

When you are playing from the tee, you should tee-up higher than you usually would. Indeed, going with a 3-wood rather than your driver may be a good strategy. This will ensure the ball gets up in the air faster, enabling you to make the most of the helping wind. Besides, most amateurs tend to hit a 3-wood more consistently well than their driver. For an approach shot, or a tee shot into a par three, you will require less club than usual, in proportion to the strength of the wind.

Playing with the wind behind you tends to minimize the amount of spin you put on the ball: either sidespin to the left or the right or backspin. Allow for the ball to run more on landing than it usually would. Playing with the wind makes it also difficult to stop the ball on the green or indeed to control a less than full approach shot. For that reason, leave yourself a full pitch into the flag rather than try to finesse a half-wedge downwind.

The Shot in a Left-to-Right Wind

For most golfers, a cross-wind poses greater problems than a headwind. Which cross-wind they find the hardest depends on the shape of shot they normally hit. The best strategy calls for you to shape the shot into the wind, thereby reducing simultaneously the effect of the curve on your ball and the effect of the wind on it. If you are playing into a left-to-right wind, you will need to draw the ball, the technique for which we discussed on page 102.

Set up with both a closed club face and a closed stance, to shape the flight pattern. The club face should point at the target and the ball should be back in your stance. Go down the grip a little to enhance your feeling of control over the club. There is not much wrist cock with this shot, but through impact your right hand should cross over the left to impart the necessary spin. A three-quarter swing is all you need - you don't want to risk losing your balance over this shot.

Since your swing is not complete, and you have effectively taken loft off the club by going down the grip, take at least one more club, probably two, to allow for the fact that the wind will straighten out your shot and therefore reduce the distance the ball will fly. As you are hitting into the wind, the ball will sit down quickly on landing.

Alternatively, you may want to ride the wind with your ball to obtain maximum distance, particularly when hitting with your driver off the tee. Then you should fade the ball that will lead us on to the other cross-wind.

The Shot in a Right-to-Left Wind

If you want to ride this wind, and sling a draw into the right-to-left breeze, adopt the technique I have just described. Be careful, though. The combination of drawspin and the wind from the right will cause the ball to move a great deal through the air. Aim well right of where you want the ball to land. If that means aiming out-of-bounds, for example, you might want to reconsider your tactics.

More often than not, the best strategy will be to hit a left-to-right shot into this wind. Open your stance, with the ball well back in it, and choke down on the grip. Your takeaway should go back outside the line, as though you were separating your hands from your body. To keep your balance, use only a three-quarter swing and take more club to allow for the fact that the wind will knock distance off this shot.

Coming down, you should feel as if you are chopping across the ball, with negligible wrist cock. Your left hand controls the shot, so grip a little more firmly than normal with that hand. Don't let the clubhead get ahead of your hands. Beyond impact, let your left side - both hand and body - dominate the follow through.

The follow through position indicates precisely what I have tried to achieve: to hold the ball into that right-to-left wind. It also reminds me of the way Lee Trevino and Paul Azinger complete their swings. They are two of the finest left-to-right shotmakers I have ever seen.

Strategy

TROUBLE-SHOOTING

So now you've hit the ball into trouble. Real trouble. What do you do? First, adopt the right attitude. Not only do you require imagination to visualize the shot you want to play and the skill to execute it but also you need the right frame of mind. Every time you go into the woods looking for your ball after a wayward shot, and thinking that you'll find it in an unplayable lie, the chances are it will be unplayable. Having the right attitude is absolutely key.

When I hit a ball into deep trouble, as I frequently did in my 1995 Ryder Cup singles match against Tom Lehman, all I wanted, as I walked toward my ball, was an opportunity to make a swing with the club. And whenever a golfer can physically swing the club, there will be a way out, however small, be it forward, backward, left or right. The question is, how?

Before you get to your ball to ascertain its lie, you will already know the distance to the green or your next target, but for real trouble-shooting, distance may not be relevant at all. The main purpose of your next shot is to get the ball out of its present predicament.

Distance is relevant, however, in another context. If, for example, you decide your best escape route is to play out sideways to the fairway, make sure you don't take so much club - or in your desperation to get out, hit the ball so hard - that you fly the ball clean over the fairway and into the rough or some hazard on the other side. Similarly, if you elect to play out toward some other target you've chosen for your immediate purpose, such as a bunker, think carefully about what you are trying to do and how you are going to achieve this goal.

The Analysis

Once you have decided on the shot that will see you safely out of trouble, you then need to determine the likely reaction of the ball under the circumstances. The position in which it lies will have a significant effect on its flight pattern.

For example, if the ball sits on an uphill slope, you might have a chance to hit the ball high, maybe through a gap in the trees - the "window of opportunity", as I call it. If the land is sloping downhill, that option will not be practical. Your club selection must be guided by these factors.

On the final hole of the final round of the 1993 European Masters/Swiss Open, I was in the rough and the only alternative to playing out sideways was to go through a small gap in the trees. I opened the face of my pitching wedge and did just that. The shot worked. Why did I take such a risk? I will deal with that point next.

The Alternative Approach

Nick Price says that his favorite oxymoron in golf is "cautious aggression". It's a good description of the attitude I believe you should have on the course. I don't advocate daredevil shots that you cannot make work. Even golf professionals don't unnecessarily take an aggressive approach in major tournaments.

Nick Faldo, for instance, has said that he only plays a risky shot if he feels he has at least a 90 per cent chance of success. I guess my personal risk-taking factor would be nearer 80 per cent, but although I understand what Nick means, it is in fact almost impossible to assign percentages to these situations. Each case, each shot, has to be handled on its merits.

In weighing up whether you should take the riskier option or take the cautious approach, you should take into account what hole you are on, which round it is, and your position in the tournament or competition you are playing in. The situation may also be different if you are competing at match play as opposed to stroke play, and in the case of the former, you need to consider how your opponent is placed.

If you play out safely sideways, you may then have a 7-iron shot into the green. If you take the riskier route and are successful, you may still need a wedge to get home. Either way, you can't do better than be on the green in three strokes. In that case, the only benefit you can reap from the risky option is a wedge shot as compared to a 7-iron approach. In other words, it's not worth taking a risk that may leave you eventually reaching the green in six strokes or more if you fail.

In the 1993 European Masters/Swiss Open at Crans-sur-Sierre, I had played a difficult and highly risky wedge shot back into play on the final hole of the tournament. I left the ball about 30 yards from the flag after two shots on this short par four, and I needed a birdie to have a chance of winning. With a bunker between my ball and the hole, success didn't look likely. I clipped the shot nicely, it landed on the green and rolled into the cup. Even then, the tale did not have a happy ending for me. Barry Lane still won by one stroke.

I would not have risked that difficult wedge shot if that situation had arisen on the 10th hole, even in the last round, rather than on the final hole. It would have been too much of a gamble to risk the shot while there were still several holes to play in which to make up lost ground. But on the last hole, it was the only hope I had of winning - albeit a slim one. I had to go for it. It was then or never. I always play to win and it would not have occurred to me to chip out safely and play to finish as runner-up.

Again, you have to decide whether the risk of the bold shot is worth taking, and to do that you have to consider exactly what you want to achieve. As for the actual playing of the shot, that depends on what you need to do. In the foregoing chapters, we have looked at what you need to do to hit the ball high (as I am doing here) or low, with a draw or a fade. Apply those principles now. Be decisive with your strike at the ball and don't look up too early to see where it has gone. If you are tempted to do that, you might look down again to find that it is still in some bush or twigs just in front of your feet.

The Drop under Penalty

When considering whether you should play a very risky shot, you should also figure out what the consequences of taking a drop under penalty for an unplayable lie would be. Under the Rules of Golf, most recently revised by the Royal & Ancient Golf Club of St. Andrews and the United States Golf Association effective January 1, 1996, this is dealt with under Rule 28. It is worth quoting in full.

"The player may declare his ball unplayable at any place on the course except when the ball is in a water hazard. [For this situation, see Chapter 6.] The player is the sole judge as to whether his ball is unplayable.

If the player deems his ball to be unplayable, he shall, under penalty of one stroke:

a. Play a ball as nearly as possible at the spot from which the original ball was last played (see Rule 20-5); or

b. Drop a ball within two club-lengths of the spot where the ball lay, but not nearer the hole; or

c. Drop a ball behind the point where the ball lay, keeping that point directly between the hole and the spot on which the ball

OPPOSITE: *The lie may look unpromising, but before deciding whether you are going to attempt to play the ball as it lies, you have to weigh up the consequences, and they may vary depending on which hole you are playing, whether this is match play or stroke play, the state of your match or round, and what your options would be if you elected to take a drop under penalty.*
OVERLEAF: *Before deciding what to do, look to see if there is what I call a "window of opportunity". In this case, there is a gap in the trees that, depending on how the ball is lying, might prove a better option - maybe both more rewarding than a drop under penalty and less risky than trying to play out sideways. Always consider all the circumstances before playing your shot, bearing in mind not only the factors I mentioned before but also the limits of your own capabilities.*

is dropped, with no limit to how far behind that point the ball may be dropped.

If the unplayable ball is in a bunker, the player may proceed under Clause a, b or c. If he elects to proceed under Clause b or c, a ball must be dropped in the bunker.

The ball may be cleaned when lifted under this Rule."

The respective penalties for a breach of this Rule are loss of hole in match play and two strokes in stroke play.

The first of those choices requires you to go back to where you hit the first ball from (Rule 20-5). You therefore have to weigh up where the two-club Rule would leave you dropping the ball, and if that would leave you better placed; or if the third option would afford you the most generous opportunity for relief.

You have to decide whether any of those alternatives is better than having a bash at the ball as it lies. Only you can decide that, depending on the state of your match or your round, and on your own abilities. You will note that under the Rules, the choice is entirely yours. Your opponent or partner has no say in the matter. And don't forget to take advantage of the opportunity afforded under this Rule to check if there is any dirt or other matter on the ball and clean it accordingly.

By taking a one-shot penalty, you may now be able to go for the green. I remember that in the first round of the 1988 Open at Royal Lytham & St. Annes, which I went on to win, I took a penalty drop for an unplayable lie at each of the 14th and 18th holes, both tough par fours. I bogeyed both of them but still shot 67.

The five at the 14th was a good example of what I have just been talking about. I hooked my second shot into some bushes well left and short of the green. Having considered what I should do, I chose option c. Keeping in line with the point where my ball had been, I eventually dropped my ball some 125 yards from the hole. Now playing my fourth shot, I struck a 7-iron to 15 feet and rolled the putt in. Nothing to it!

Taking a one-shot penalty for an unplayable lie might enable you to be on the green of a par four hole in three shots, with a chance of saving your par. Even if you pull off your escape shot from the trees and get the ball back on to the fairway in two, you can't do any better than that.

The Alternative Approach

RIGHT, OPPOSITE AND OVERLEAF: *Here I am aiming for the "window of opportunity" to attempt this shot, you want to be sure that the ball is lying well enough to get it up in the air, and that the ground is in your favor, too. An uphill lie would be helpful. Do not even think of trying this shot if the ball is lying poorly or on a downhill slope. Once you are confident that those elements are in your favor, go for it, learning from the lessons we have been through earlier in this book. Keep your balance, and once you've made the commitment to play the shot, be decisive in the way you hit it.*